SCHOLASTIC

National Curricul...

MATHS
Revision Guide

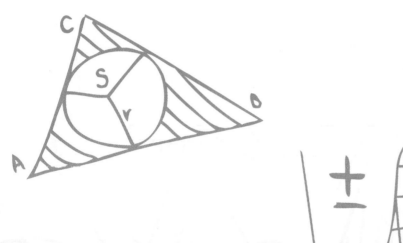

✓ Recap
✓ Revise
✓ Skills Check

Ages 8–9
Year 4

KS2

National Curriculum
MATHS
Revision Guide

Book End, Range Road, Witney, Oxfordshire, OX29 0YD
Registered office: Westfield Road, Southam, Warwickshire CV47 0RA
www.scholastic.co.uk

© 2016, Scholastic Ltd

1 2 3 4 5 6 7 8 9   6 7 8 9 0 1 2 3 4 5

British Library Cataloguing-in-Publication Data
A catalogue record for this book is available from the British Library.

ISBN 978-1407-15988-1
Printed in Italy by STIGE – Turin

Author
Paul Hollin

Editorial
Rachel Morgan, Jenny Wilcox, Mark Walker, Mary Nathan, Christine Vaughan, Kate Pedlar, Janette Ratcliffe and Julia Roberts

Series Design
Scholastic Design Team: Nicolle Thomas and Neil Salt

Design
Oxford Designers & Illustrators

Cover Design
Scholastic Design Team: Nicolle Thomas and Neil Salt

Cover Illustration
Shutterstock / © VIGE.CO

Illustration
Matt Ward, Bee Hive Illustration

Contents

Contents

How to use this book

Introduction

This book has been written to help children reinforce the mathematics they have learned at school. It provides information and varied examples, activities and questions in a clear and consistent format across 34 units, covering all of the National Curriculum for Mathematics for this age group.

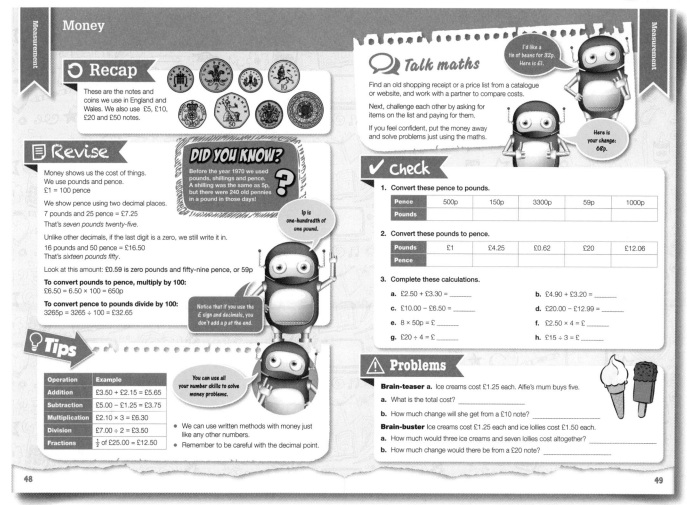

Unit structure

- **Recap** – a recap of basic facts of the mathematical area in focus.
- **Revise** – examples and facts specific to the age group.
- **Tips** – short and simple advice to aid understanding.
- **Talk maths** – focused activities that encourage verbal practice.
- **Check** – a focused range of questions, with answers at the end of the book.
- **Problems** – word problems requiring mathematics to be used in context.

Keep some blank or squared paper handy for notes and calculations!

Using this book at home

Improving your child's maths

It sounds obvious, but this is the best reason for using this book. Whether working sequentially through units, dipping in to resolve confusion, or reinforcing classroom learning, you can use this book to help your child see the benefits and pleasures of being competent in maths.

Consolidating school work

Most schools communicate clearly what they are doing each week via newsletters or homework. Using this book, alongside the maths being done at school, can boost children's mastery of the concepts.

Be sure not to get ahead of schoolwork or to confuse your child. If in doubt, talk to your child's class teacher.

Revising for tests

Regular testing is a fact of life for children these days, like it or not. Improving children's confidence is a good way to avoid stress as well as improve performance. Where children have obvious difficulties, dipping in to the book and focusing on specific facts and skills can be very helpful. To provide specific practice for end-of-year tests we recommend *National Curriculum Maths Tests for Year 4*.

Tips for effective home learning

Do a little, often

Keep sessions to an absolute maximum of 30 minutes. Even if children want to keep going, short amounts of focused study on a regular basis will help to sustain learning and enthusiasm in the long run.

Track progress

The revision tracker chart on page 7 provides a simple way for children to record their progress

with this book. Remember, you've really 'got it' when you can understand and apply the maths confidently in different contexts. This means all the questions in the *Check* and *Problems* sections should not present any difficulties.

Avoid confusion

If your child really doesn't seem to understand a particular unit, take a step back. There may be some prior knowledge that s/he does not understand, or it may contradict how they have learned similar facts at school. Try looking at much simpler examples than those given in the book, and if in doubt talk to your child's teacher.

Talk, talk, talk

There is big value in discussing maths, both using vocabulary and explaining concepts. The more children can be encouraged to do this, especially explaining their thinking and understanding, the better the learning. Even if adults understand the work better than children, having them 'teach' you is a great way to consolidate their learning.

Practice makes perfect

Even the world's best footballers have to regularly practise kicking a ball. Brief warm ups before starting a unit, such as rapid recall of times tables or addition facts, or answering a few questions on mathematical vocabulary (see glossary) can help keep children on their toes.

Maths is everywhere – use it!

Children have lots of English lessons at school, and they use language almost constantly in daily life. They also have lots of maths lessons but encounter its use in daily life much less. Involving children in everyday maths is very useful. Shopping and money are the obvious ones, but cooking, decorating, planning holidays, catching buses, to name a few examples, can all involve important mathematical thinking and talk.

Revision tracker

	Not sure	Getting there	Got it!
Read, write, order and compare numbers with up to four digits			
Round any number to the nearest 10, 100 or 1000			
Count in steps of 6, 7, 9, 25 and 1000			
Count backwards through zero to include negative numbers			
Understand Roman numerals up to 100			
Use mental methods for addition and subtraction			
Use written methods for addition			
Use written methods for subtraction			
Recall and use times tables facts for tables to 12 × 12			
Use mental methods for multiplication and division			
Use written methods for short multiplication			
Use written methods for short division			
Recognise and use equivalent fractions			
Add and subtract simple fractions			
Write tenths and hundredths in fraction and decimal form			
Convert fractions to decimals			
Compare and round numbers with up to two decimal places			
Convert between different units of measurement			
Solve problems involving time			
Convert between analogue time and digital time			
Convert between 12-hour clock time and 24-hour clock time			
Solve problems involving money			
Solve problems involving mass and capacity			
Solve problems involving length and distance			
Measure and calculate the perimeters of shapes			
Count squares to find the area of shapes			
Compare, order and name different angles up to two right angles			
Name and classify different triangles			
Name and classify different quadrilaterals			
Identify lines of symmetry in 2D shapes			
Read and plot coordinates			
Translate points on a graph			
Interpret information in tables and pictograms			
Create and use bar charts			
Create and use simple time graphs			

Numbers to 9999

The value of a digit depends on which column it is in.

↺ Recap

Our number system uses 100s, 10s and 1s.
265 in words is two hundred and sixty-five.

100s	10s	1s
2	6	5

The **place value** of the digit 2 is 100s. The digit 2 represents 200.
The **place value** of the digit 6 is 10s. The digit 6 represents 60.
The **place value** of the digit 5 is 1s. The digit 5 represents 5.

📋 Revise

This number is five thousand, seven hundred and nine.

1000s	100s	10s	1s
5	7	0	9

Zeros are important. They help to show the place value of all the digits.

We can write numbers in words or using numerals.

- six thousand, four hundred and eighty-five ⟶ 6485
- three thousand, nine hundred and one ⟶ 3901
- two thousand and seven ⟶ 2007

💡 Tips

- When you're asked to write a number, write the place values above the digits if you're stuck.
  Say this number. 8704
  Write the place values above the digits.

1000s	100s	10s	1s
8	7	0	4

The number is eight thousand, seven hundred and four.

DID YOU KNOW?

A thousand is ten hundreds.

Talk maths

What are the biggest and smallest numbers you can make?

0 1 2 3 4 5 6 7 8 9

Write the digits 0 to 9 on some pieces of card or paper. Use them to make ten different 4-digit numbers. Write them down, and then read them aloud.

✔ Check

1. Write these numbers in words.

    a. 7380 _____

    b. 2069 _____

2. Write these numbers in digits.

    a. six thousand, eight hundred and forty-one _____

    b. five thousand and two _____

3. Arrange these numbers in order, from smallest to largest.

    1612   5000   725   8   250   3875   92   9999

    _____ _____ _____ _____ _____ _____ _____ _____

4. Complete this chart.

1000 more	3350				
Number	2350	1243	4789	7000	8999
1000 less	1350				

⚠ Problems

Blinkton	Dipton	Mumsford	Pilbery	Wester
4307	974	3824	1092	1003

Five villages count their populations.

Brain-teaser a. Which village has the smallest population? _____

b. Which village has the largest population? _____

Brain-buster The number of people living in all the villages, added together, is 11,200.

Write this in words. _____

Estimating and rounding

↻ Recap

We sometimes have to round numbers. This can help us to estimate amounts and calculations more easily.

To round a number to the nearest 10 we look at its position on the number line.

We then look for the nearest 10.

- 12 rounds down to 10.
- 18 rounds up to 20.
- 15 is halfway, but we always round it up.

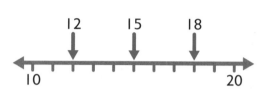

🖹 Revise

We can also round large numbers to the nearest 100 or 1000.

432 rounds down to 400.

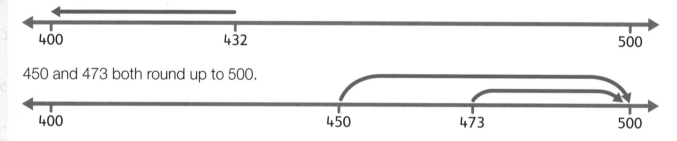

450 and 473 both round up to 500.

1268 rounds down to 1000.

1500 and 1647 both round up to 2000.

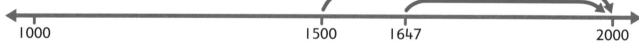

💡 Tips

We can round numbers to give a quick estimate. This is useful for seeing if your answers are about right.
So, for 372 + 221, a quick estimate is 400 + 200 = 600.

- Think carefully about what you want to round to: 10s, 100s or 1000s.
  - 6852 rounds to the nearest 10 as 6850.
  - 6852 rounds to the nearest 100 as 6900.
  - 6852 rounds to the nearest 1000 as 7000.

💬 Talk maths

What is 45 rounded to the nearest 10?

Write down six different numbers between 0 and 9999. For example:

| 45 | 94 | 143 | 2530 | 5265 | 9250 |

Work with a partner and challenge each other to round the numbers.

What is 2530 rounded to the nearest 1000?

✔ Check

1. Round each number to the nearest 10, 100 and 1000.

	To the nearest 10	To the nearest 100	To the nearest 1000
a. 77			
b. 583			
c. 1232			
d. 3765			

2. Estimate to the nearest 10. Round each number before you add.

   a. 43 + 36 _____   **b.** 25 + 36 _____   **c.** 82 + 37 _____

3. Estimate to the nearest 100. Round each number before you add.

   a. 423 + 186 _____   **b.** 75 + 215 _____   **c.** 452 + 821 _____

4. Estimate to the nearest 1000. Round each number before you add.

   a. 4233 + 1836 _____   **b.** 825 + 3336 _____   **c.** 7852 + 3500 _____

⚠ Problems

Blinkton	Dipton	Mumsford	Pilbery	Wester
4307	974	3824	1092	1003

Brain-teaser
Look at these different village populations.
Which villages have populations that are 4000, when rounded to the nearest 1000?

_____

Brain-buster Estimate the total number of people living in all five villages to the nearest 1000.

_____

Counting in steps

1	2	3	4	5	6	7	8	9	10
11	12	13	14	15	16	17	18	19	20
21	22	23	24	25	26	27	28	29	30
31	32	33	34	35	36	37	38	39	40
41	42	43	44	45	46	47	48	49	50
51	52	53	54	55	56	57	58	59	60
61	62	63	64	65	66	67	68	69	70
71	72	73	74	75	76	77	78	79	80
81	82	83	84	85	86	87	88	89	90
91	92	93	94	95	96	97	98	99	100

↺ Recap

When we count in steps, we add or subtract the same number each time. In this 100-square all the multiples of 4 have been shaded.

Can you count in steps of 5? Shade each multiple of 5 the same colour.

Which numbers are multiples of 4 **and** 5?

📋 Revise

Use the 100-square above to count in steps of 6, 7 and 9.

0	6	12	18	24	30	36	42	48…
0	7	14	21	28	35	42	49	56…
0	9	18	27	36	45	54	63	72…

Try colouring in these steps on the 100-square.

You can count in steps of any number. You need to learn to do this with 25s and 1000s.

0	25	50	75	100	125	150
0	1000	2000	3000	4000	5000	

Can you see any patterns?

Can you keep these sequences going?

Remember that counting in steps and times tables facts have lots in common.

💡 Tips

- 6 + 6 + 6 is 'three lots of 6', or 3 × 6. They all equal 18.
- 7 + 7 + 7 + 7 + 7 + 7 + 7 + 7 + 7 is 'nine lots of 7', or 9 × 7. They all equal 63.
- 9 + 9 + 9 + 9 + 9 is 'five lots of 9', or 5 × 9. They all equal 45.

Talk maths

Try racing against the clock. What is the fastest you can count aloud in 6s, 7s and 9s up to 100 without making a mistake?

What about counting in 25s up to 300?

Or counting in 1000s up to 10,000?

✔ Check

1. **Complete these sequences.**

   a. Count on in steps of 6.   **36,** _____ , _____ , _____ , _____

   b. Count on in steps of 7.   **56,** _____ , _____ , _____ , _____

   c. Count on in steps of 9.   **45,** _____ , _____ , _____ , _____

   d. Count on in steps of 25.   **350,** _____ , _____ , _____ , _____

   e. Count on in steps of 1000.   **2000,** _____ , _____ , _____ , _____

2. **Complete these sequences.**

   a. Count back in steps of 6.   **90, 84,** _____ , _____ , _____ , _____

   b. Count back in steps of 7.   **77, 70,** _____ , _____ , _____ , _____

   c. Count back in steps of 9.   **81, 72,** _____ , _____ , _____ , _____

   d. Count back in steps of 25.   **875,** _____ , _____ , _____ , _____

   e. Count back in steps of 1000.   **9000,** _____ , _____ , _____ , _____

⚠ Problems

Brain-teaser Joe saves £6 a week for eight weeks. Kate saves £9 a week for five weeks. Who has the most money, and how much more do they have?

_____

Brain-buster Kate's older sister wants to save £800 for a holiday abroad. If she can save £25 a week, how long will she have to save for?

_____

Negative numbers

↺ Recap

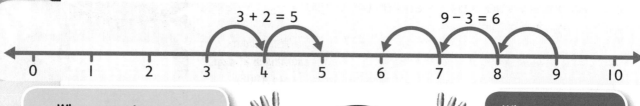

$$3 + 2 = 5 \qquad 9 - 3 = 6$$

0 1 2 3 4 5 6 7 8 9 10

When we **count on** we move to the right along the number line.
$3 + 2 = 5$

When we **count back** we move to the left.
$9 - 3 = 6$

📄 Revise

Numbers can be negative as well as positive.

−5 −4 −3 −2 −1 0 1 2 3 4 5

Look at the numbers on each side of zero.
On the right, the more you move away from zero, the bigger the numbers get (5 is bigger than 2).
On the left, the more you move away from zero, the smaller the numbers get (−2 is bigger than −5).

We can count back through zero. Use the number line to count back in steps of 1.

Start at 1 and count back 2. You should stop at −1.
Start at 2 and count back 4. You should stop at −2.
Start at 4 and count back 7. You should stop at −3.
Start at 1 and count back 5. You should stop at −4.
Start at 3 and count back 8. You should stop at −5.

DID YOU KNOW?

°C means degrees Celsius. Zero degrees Celsius is the temperature at which water freezes.

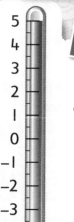

5
4
3
2
1
0
−1
−2
−3
−4
−5

💡 Tips

Notice that when you count in steps below zero, you still count in order.

- Temperature is a great way to practise counting back through zero.

If you start at 5°C and count back 5°C, you end at 0°C.

If you start at 2°C and count back 10°C, you stop at −8°C.

💬 Talk maths

Draw a thermometer, as large as you can, and mark its scale from –10°C to 10°C. Ask someone to check that you have written the scale correctly.

Working with someone, place a small object or counter somewhere on the scale of the thermometer. Challenge your partner to count on or back.

If you want to make this harder, don't mention the temperature and just present your challenges as subtractions.

> **Count back 7 from 3°C.**

> **3°C, count back 7, stops at –4°C.**

✔ Check

–10 –9 –8 –7 –6 –5 –4 –3 –2 –1 0 1 2 3 4 5 6 7 8 9 10

1. **Use the number line to help you solve these problems.**

   a. 6 count back 5 = _____   b. 3 count back 4 = _____

   c. 1 count back 4 = _____   d. 2 count back 7 = _____

   e. 0 count back 5 = _____   f. 5 count back 10 = _____

   g. 8 count back 9 = _____   h. 10 count back 16 = _____

2. **Say how many steps have been counted back on each number line.**

   a.
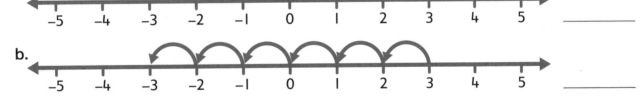
   –5 –4 –3 –2 –1 0 1 2 3 4 5 _____

   b.
   –5 –4 –3 –2 –1 0 1 2 3 4 5 _____

   c.

   –5 –4 –3 –2 –1 0 1 2 3 4 5 _____

⚠ Problems

Brain-teaser The temperature starts at 2°C, and then goes down 3°C. What is the new temperature? _____

Brain-buster The temperature drops from 9°C to –6°C. How many degrees has it dropped by? _____

15

Roman numerals

↻ Recap

In our number system, all of our numbers are made using ten different digits.

0 1 2 3 4 5 6 7 8 9

Using place value (100s, 10s and 1s), we can use these ten digits to represent any number we wish.

Revise

There are many different number systems. One other that we still use is Roman numerals. The Romans used letters to represent some numbers.

There are five Roman numerals that you need to know.

I (1)   **V** (5)   **X** (10)   **L** (50)   **C** (100)

By using these numbers together, they could make any number, but it isn't always easy! The chart below can help you to learn Roman numerals to 100.

Number	1	2	3	4	5	6	7	8	9	10
Roman numeral	I	II	III	IV	V	VI	VII	VIII	IX	X
Number	11	12	13	14	15	16	17	18	19	20
Roman numeral	XI	XII	XIII	XIV	XV	XVI	XVII	XVIII	XIX	XX
Number	30	40	50	60	70	80	90	100		
Roman numeral	XXX	XL	L	LX	LXX	LXXX	XC	C		

💡 Tips

XCIV plus LIX equals...

- It all seems very complicated, but if you learn some important numbers it can be okay.
- Learn the Roman numerals 1 to 10 by heart. It will make other numbers easier to understand.
- Also, pay close attention to how they make 4 (IV), 9 (IX), 40 (XL) and 90 (CX).

Talk maths

Challenge each other to write your ages in Roman numerals.

I I I V X X X L C

Make a set of Roman numeral cards. It is important to have three 'one' cards, and three 'ten' cards. These can make any number between 1 and 100.
Next, challenge a friend to make numbers. You can either call out a number, such as seventy-three, or arrange some Roman numerals.
Whenever anyone gives an answer, they must explain their working out.

✔ Check

1. Change these numbers to Roman numerals.

   a. 4 _____ b. 11 _____ c. 25 _____ d. 19 _____

   e. 52 _____ f. 45 _____ g. 90 _____ h. 87 _____

2. Change these Roman numerals to numbers.

   a. VI _____ b. IX _____ c. XVII _____ d. XXII _____

   e. LV _____ f. XL _____ g. LXXXVIII _____ h. XC _____

3. Which digit can't be shown with Roman numerals?

   _____

⚠ Problems

Change these Roman numerals into numbers, and then complete the calculations.

Brain-teaser XIV plus XXIII

Brain-buster XCI minus LXV

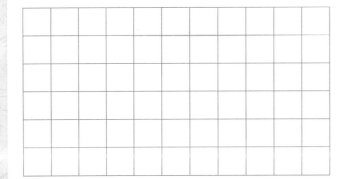
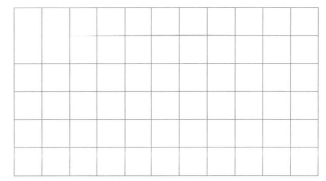

17

Mental methods for addition and subtraction

And, you can use these facts to do harder mental calculations. 70 + 80 = 150, 700 + 800 = 1500

↻ Recap

You will probably know how to do some calculations in your head, and also how to do them by writing on paper. You must know your number bonds. Each number bond gives you four different facts.

Look at these.
| 7 + 8 = 15 | 8 + 7 = 15 | 15 − 8 = 7 | 15 − 7 = 8 |

📄 Revise

And this means that 12 + 25 = 37, 37 − 25 = 12 and 37 − 12 = 25.

Here are two very useful mental methods.

Partitioning a number into 10s and 1s is useful: 25 + 12 = 25 + 10 + 2 = 35 + 2 = 37

25 26 27 28 29 30 31 32 33 34 35 36 37

Bridging is used when one number is close to a 10.
For example, for 75 + 98, instead of adding 98, add 100 and then subtract 2.

+100

−2

75   173   175

You can use both of these methods for subtraction too.

So, 75 + 98 = 75 + 100 − 2 = 173.

| 38 − 13 = 38 − 10 − 3 = 25 | 46 − 9 = 46 − 10 + 1 = 37 |
| 57 − 24 = 57 − 20 − 4 = 33 | 246 − 97 = 246 − 100 + 3 = 149 |

💡 Tips

Remember, if in doubt, write it out!

- Look carefully at calculations before you try to solve them in your head – you might prefer to solve them with a written calculation. Look at the calculations below, which ones would you solve mentally?

| 25 + 96 | 645 + 377 | 89 − 30 | 204 − 157 |

Talk maths

Demonstrate to an adult how to use different mental methods for addition and subtraction. Remind them that the first thing to decide is whether a mental method is appropriate or not.

Use the calculations in the box to get you started.

Calculation	OK for mental methods?
23 + 11	yes
47 + 98	yes
645 + 123	yes
472 + 687	maybe not!
35 – 9	yes
642 – 102	yes
743 – 510	yes
403 – 187	maybe not!

✔ Check

1. Add these numbers, using mental methods.

   a. 36 + 14 = ____ b. 64 + 25 = ____ c. 95 + 13 = ____ d. 343 + 51 = ____

   e. 12 + 11 = ____ f. 67 + 19 = ____ g. 67 + 28 = ____ h. 467 + 97 = ____

2. Subtract these numbers, using mental methods.

   a. 27 – 13 = ____ b. 64 – 22 = ____ c. 90 – 46 = ____ d. 357 – 206 = ____

   e. 45 – 9 = ____ f. 72 – 11 = ____ g. 65 – 19 = ____ h. 436 – 198 = ____

3. Solve these calculations using mental methods.

   a. 43 + 34 = ____ b. 67 + 32 = ____ c. 335 + 150 = ____ d. 2231 + 3607 = ____

   e. 86 – 24 = ____ f. 54 – 33 = ____ g. 276 – 143 = ____ h. 5493 – 3170 = ____

⚠ Problems

Brain-teaser

a. Tina has £47 in her bank account, and she receives another £52 for her birthday.
   How much does she have altogether? _____

b. James is travelling from London to Newcastle. The distance is 295 miles.
   So far he has travelled 190 miles. How far does he have to go? _____

Brain-buster

Joe's mum buys a new car. The car costs £4500 and she pays a deposit of £2200.
How much does she still have to pay? _____

Written methods for addition

↻ Recap

There are formal written methods for adding numbers. You may have been taught methods a bit different to this one. You should use whichever method you are comfortable with.

We arrange the numbers so that the place value of their digits line up.

	100s	10s	1s
	1	4	5
+	3	2	7
	4	7	2
		1	

> That's why some people call it column addition. The secret is to add the digits in each column like 1s. Remember to add on any numbers that have been carried.

📋 Revise

The biggest digit we can write in a column is 9. If the digits in the 1s column add up to more than 10, we must carry the 10 to the next column, and leave the 1s behind. You can do the same when adding digits in the other columns.

	2	4	6	1
+	1	5	7	8
	4	0	3	9
		1		1

Sometimes the digits add up exactly to 10. In this calculation, we carry one 10 an leave no 1s behind. In the 100s column, we carry one 1000 and leave no 100s behind.

	3	2	7	4
+	2	8	1	6
	6	0	9	0
		1		1

💡 Tips

- Remember to carry any 10s, 100s or 1000s to the next column.

> You can add as many numbers as you want using column addition.

	1	3	5	2
	2	8	1	5
		6	3	4
+	3	0	2	5
	7	8	2	6
		1	1	1

Talk maths

Look at this addition and explain it aloud. Say what is happening at each stage. Make sure you work in the correct order, right to left.

	4	8	6	7
+	2	5	0	8
	7	3	7	5

Try some column additions using three or four numbers, explaining each stage to someone you know.

✔ Check

1. Complete each of these additions.

a.
	2	3	7
+	4	8	1

b.
	7	4	6
+	2	5	7

c.
	2	4	2	6
+	1	4	8	5

d.
	1	3	2	7
	2	4	5	1
+	3	8	0	6

2. Complete these additions. Use a written method on squared paper.

a. 365 + 237   b. 467 + 259   c. 4459 + 3557   d. 2406 + 2205 + 3670 + 1338

⚠ Problems

Brain-teaser

This chart shows the number of people attending three village fetes.

Village	Plink	Plank	Plonk
Number of visitors	825	936	89

What is the total number of visitors to the three fetes? _____

Brain-buster

This chart shows the number of fans at three rock concerts.

Band	Crush	Push	Mush
Fans	6455	7106	3453

What is the total number of fans at the three concerts? _____

Written methods for subtraction

↻ Recap

There are formal written methods for subtracting numbers. You may have been taught methods a bit different from this one. You should use whichever method you are comfortable with.

$$
\begin{array}{r}
{}^5\cancel{6}\quad {}^{13}\cancel{4}\quad {}^1 5 \\
-\quad 2\quad 7\quad 8 \\
\hline
3\quad 6\quad 7 \\
\end{array}
$$

Notice how we exchange 100s for 10s and 10s for 1s.

🗒 Revise

Just like with addition, we can use the place-value columns to subtract larger numbers.

$$
\begin{array}{r}
{}^5\cancel{6}\quad {}^1 2\quad {}^4\cancel{5}\quad {}^1 4 \\
-\quad 1\quad 7\quad 3\quad 8 \\
\hline
4\quad 5\quad 1\quad 6 \\
\end{array}
$$

You need to be very careful at each stage of a written subtraction. Look at this one.

$$
\begin{array}{r}
{}^5\cancel{6}\quad {}^{9}\cancel{\cancel{0}}\quad {}^1 4\quad 5 \\
-\quad 3\quad 1\quad 7\quad 2 \\
\hline
2\quad 8\quad 7\quad 3 \\
\end{array}
$$

Look carefully at what you must do if you want to borrow a number when the next column has a zero.

Here are some top tips for accurate subtraction work!

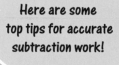

💡 Tips

- Check your subtractions by adding your answer to the number you subtracted.
- Try to estimate your answer before you start. It will help you to know if your answer is 'about right'.
- You can't have lots of subtractions in a list the way you can with additions. If you have to subtract two or three numbers, you must subtract one number and then subtract the next number from the answer.

You have to borrow from the 1000s to ten 100s, then borrow one 100 to get ten 10s.

Talk maths

Look at this subtraction and explain it aloud. Say what is happening at each stage. Make sure you work in the correct order, right to left.

```
   '2  ''2  '3   8
 -  1   3   5   6
    _____
        8   8   2
```

✔ Check

1. Complete each of these subtractions.

a.
```
   3 6 5
 - 1 4 7
 _____
```

b.
```
   6 5 3
 - 2 2 8
 _____
```

c.
```
   3 2 7
 - 1 6 5
 _____
```

d.
```
   4 7 2 5
 - 1 9 0 7
 _____
```

2. Complete each of these subtractions using a written method on squared paper.

a. 415 – 236   b. 824 – 375   c. 3542 – 937   d. 6042 – 3555

⚠ Problems

Brain-teaser

This chart shows the number of people attending three village fetes.

Village	Plink	Plank	Plonk
Number of visitors	825	936	89

a. How many more people went to Plink than Plonk? _____

b. How many more people went to Plank than Plink? _____

Brain-buster

This chart shows the number of fans at three rock concerts.

Band	Crush	Push	Mush
Fans	6455	7106	3453

If the fans of Push and Mush are combined, how many more people are there than fans of Crush? _____

23

Times tables facts

×	1	2	3	4	5	6	7	8	9	10	11	12
1	1	2	3	4	5	6	7	8	9	10	11	12
2	2	4	6	8	10	12	14	16	18	20	22	24
3	3	6	9	12	15	18	21	24	27	30	33	36
4	4	8	12	16	20	24	28	32	36	40	44	48
5	5	10	15	20	25	30	35	40	45	50	55	60
6	6	12	18	24	30	36	42	48	54	60	66	72
7	7	14	21	28	35	42	49	56	63	70	77	84
8	8	16	24	32	40	48	56	64	72	80	88	96
9	9	18	27	36	45	54	63	72	81	90	99	108
10	10	20	30	40	50	60	70	80	90	100	110	120
11	11	22	33	44	55	66	77	88	99	110	121	132
12	12	24	36	48	60	72	84	96	108	120	132	144

↻ Recap

You need to learn and to understand your tables.

> Remember: to use the times tables grid, you find a number on the side and a number on the top, like 3×4, and where the row and the column meet you get your answer. So $3 \times 4 = 12$, easy!

You should already know your 2-, 3-, 4-, 5-, 8- and 10-times tables. Use the times tables grid to check your knowledge.

We can also check divisions on the grid, because division is the inverse of multiplication.

> $5 \times 4 = 20$, so $4 \times 5 = 20$
> $20 \div 5 = 4$, and $20 \div 4 = 5$. Three numbers, four different facts.

📋 Revise

You should now be ready to learn your 6-, 7-, 9-, 11- and 12-times tables.

Times tables are like counting in steps. Can you see these on the grid above?

6-times table:	0	6	12	18	24	30	36	42	48	54	60	66	72
7-times table:	0	7	14	21	28	35	42	49	56	63	70	77	84
9-times table:	0	9	18	27	36	45	54	63	72	81	90	99	108
11-times table:	0	11	22	33	44	55	66	77	88	99	110	121	132
12-times table:	0	12	24	36	48	60	72	84	96	108	120	132	144

> Remember that times tables are like counting in steps: $9 + 9 + 9 = 3 \times 9 = 27$

💡 Tips

- Often by looking at the 1s you can spot patterns. Look at the 9- and the 12-times tables above.
- And remember, multiplication works both ways, so if you know 6×7 you also know 7×6.

> Some tables are easier to learn than others. Most people find the 2-, 5-, 10- and 11-times tables the easiest.

Talk maths

Play *In a minute*. You will need the times tables grid and a clock or watch.
Work with a partner. Take turns asking and answering times tables questions as fast as possible.

The questioner can use a hidden times tables grid to help them check answers quickly. How many questions can players answer in one minute?

If you prefer, you can set limits, such as the 6-times table only.

DID YOU KNOW?

The times tables grid only contains 78 different facts. (That's because many of the facts are repeated, such as 7 × 8 = 8 × 7). You already know thousands of facts, surely another 78 can't be that hard…

What is 4 × 6?

What is 63 ÷ 7?

What is 8 × 11?

What is 81 ÷ 9?

What is 96 ÷ 12?

✔ Check

1. Answer these times tables questions.

   a. 3 × 7 = _____   **b.** 5 × 9 = _____   **c.** 8 × 4 = _____

2. Answer these times tables questions.

   a. 20 ÷ 5 = _____   **b.** 24 ÷ 2 = _____   **c.** 42 ÷ 7 = _____

3. Write down all the numbers in the 6-times table.

   _____

4. Write down all the numbers in the 12-times table.

   _____

5. Which numbers are in both the 6- and 12-times tables?

   _____

⚠ Problems

Brain-teaser Josie is thinking of a number.
She says it is in the 6-times table and the 7-times table. What is the number? _____

Brain-buster Jim buys nine bags of crisps for 60p each. Explain how he can use his times tables to find the total cost of the crisps, and then give the answer.

_____

Mental methods for multiplication and division

↻ Recap

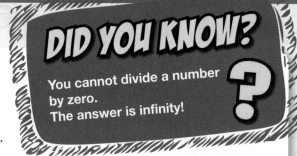
Multiplication is like repeated addition.

5 × 3 is 'five lots of 3' or 3 + 3 + 3 + 3 + 3.

Multiplication can be done in any order.

5 × 3 = 3 × 5 (answer = 15)

Division is equal sharing.

15 ÷ 3 is 15 shared into three equal lots.

Division is the inverse of multiplication.

2 × 9 = 18 so 18 ÷ 9 = 2 (and 18 ÷ 2 = 9)

And multiplication is the *inverse* of division!

📄 Revise

Some calculations can be done mentally, without writing anything down.

You should know any calculation that is in the times tables.
3 × 5 = 15   4 × 9 = 36   15 ÷ 5 = 3   36 ÷ 4 = 9

And if you know these facts you can do other calculations.
30 × 5 = 150   4 × 90 = 360   150 ÷ 5 = 30   360 ÷ 4 = 90

Multiplying by 2 is just doubling; dividing by 2 is halving.
39 × 2 = 30 + 30 + 9 + 9 = 60 + 18 = 78 $220 ÷ 2 = \frac{1}{2}$ of 200 + $\frac{1}{2}$ of 20 = 100 + 10 = 110

When you multiply or divide by 10 or 100, all the digits move one or two places in the place value table.
23 × 10 = 230   4 × 100 = 400   320 ÷ 10 = 32   600 ÷ 100 = 6

When you multiply three numbers, they can be done in any order. It's easiest to multiply by the smallest number last.
2 × 6 × 8 = 2 × 48 = 96

Don't forget: anything multiplied by 1 remains the same, and anything multiplied by zero will equal zero.

💡 Tips

If you are feeling confident, you can mix and match the mental methods shown above. Look at these.

- 50 × 30 is the same as <u>5 × 10</u> × <u>3 × 10</u>.
  Swap the order = <u>5 × 3</u> × <u>10 × 10</u> = 15 × 100 = 1500.
- 6200 ÷ 20 is done in two stages. 6200 ÷ 10 = 620,
  and then divide by 2 to give 620 ÷ 2 = 310.

Talk maths

Look at the different mental methods shown on the page opposite. Using a pencil and paper, secretly write down a few multiplications and divisions using the methods, or use the ones in this box.

Read each calculation aloud to a partner and challenge them solve it. If they make errors, explain where they went wrong.

6×8 $72 \div 9$ 150×2

$800 \div 100$ $320 \div 10$

12×200

20×30 $4 \times 5 \times 6$

$60 \div 30$ $10 \times 20 \times 30$

$160 \div 20$ $120 \div 40$

✔ Check

1. Solve these multiplications mentally.

   a. $36 \times 2 =$ _____

   b. $2 \times 2 \times 6 =$ _____

   c. $95 \times 10 =$ _____

   d. $3 \times 100 =$ _____

   e. $36 \times 20 =$ _____

   f. $3 \times 400 =$ _____

   g. $2 \times 4 \times 300 =$ _____

   h. $50 \times 90 \times 2 =$ _____

2. Solve these divisions mentally.

   a. $26 \div 2 =$ _____

   b. $64 \div 8 =$ _____

   c. $150 \div 10 =$ _____

   d. $3000 \div 100 =$ _____

   e. $120 \div 10 =$ _____

   f. $60 \div 20 =$ _____

   g. $300 \div 15 =$ _____

   h. $640 \div 80 =$ _____

⚠ Problems

Brain-teaser There are 120 children in a school.

a. If they each spend 20p at the tuck shop, how much money is collected altogether? _____

b. If the children are divided equally into 10 groups, how many will be in each group? _____

Brain-buster There are 120 children in a school.

a. If each child spends 20p at the tuck shop every day for three days, how much money will be collected altogether? _____

b. If the children are divided equally into 30 groups, how many will be in each group? _____

Written methods for short multiplication

↻ Recap

We know that multiplication is repeated addition.
$4 \times 7 = 7 + 7 + 7 + 7 = 28$

We have also looked at some mental methods for doing multiplications in your head.
$12 \times 20 = 12 \times 10 \times 2 = 120 \times 2 = 240$

Sometimes calculations are just too hard to do in your head.
1247×6

That's when it's time to use a **formal written method**.

📄 Revise

We call this short multiplication.

We know that our number system uses these place-value columns: 1000s, 100s, 10s and 1s.

To make multiplication easier, we can use formal written methods using these columns.

When multiplying a larger number by a number less than 10, you must multiply each digit at the top by the single digit. If necessary, exchange 1s, 10s or 100s, and then add them.

Notice how $4 \times 5 = 20$. We carry the two 10s and leave zero 1s in the 1s column. Also $4 \times 3 = 12$. We carry the one 100, then in the 10s column we add the two carried 10s to the two 10s and write 4 in this column. $4 \times 2 = 8$ but we need to add the carried 100 which makes 9, so we write 9 in the 100s column. So the answer is 940.

		2	3	5
×				4
		9	4	0
			1	2

💡 Tips

Make sure you know your times tables facts!

- To carry out short multiplication, you still need to know your multiplication facts.
- And don't forget, you can estimate your answer. Use this to check that your formal written method gives you the size of answer you expect.

  For example, 124×6 will be a more than 720 but less than 780.
  $(6 \times 120 = 720, 6 \times 130 = 780)$

Talk maths

Remember: you still have to multiply zeros, and anything times zero is... zero!

Look at the short multiplications below and explain them aloud. Say how each stage was done.

a.
```
        3   4
    ×       4
    ─────────
    1   3   6
            1
```

b.
```
        4   6   2
    ×           6
    ─────────────
    2   7   7   2
        3       1
```

✔ Check

1. Complete each of these short multiplications.

   a.
   ```
       3 8
   ×     3
   ───────
   
   ───────
   ```

   b.
   ```
     4 5 7
   ×     2
   ───────
   
   ───────
   ```

   c.
   ```
     3 4 2
   ×     4
   ───────
   
   ───────
   ```

   d.
   ```
     8 0 6
   ×     5
   ───────
   
   ───────
   ```

2. Complete these calculations using a written method for short multiplication.

   a. 153 × 3   b. 267 × 2   c. 538 × 4   d. 1273 × 6

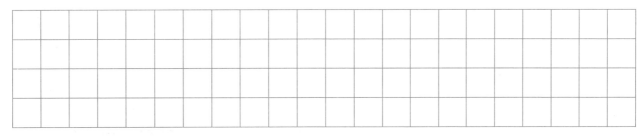

⚠ Problems

Brain-teaser A school's tuck shop sells muesli bars for 7p each.

143 bars are sold. How much money is collected? _____

Brain-buster The school tuck shop also sells cartons of juice for 20p each.

125 children buy a muesli bar and a carton of juice.
How much money is collected altogether? _____

Written methods for short division

↻ Recap

Dividing means sharing something equally. If we share six biscuits between three people, they will get two biscuits each.

We know that division is the **inverse** of multiplication, so your times tables give you lots of division facts.

$3 \times 5 = 15$, so $15 \div 3 = 5$ and $15 \div 5 = 3$

$6 \times 8 = 48$, so $48 \div 6 = 8$ and $48 \div 8 = 6$

$10 \times 12 = 120$, so $120 \div 12 = 10$ and $120 \div 10 = 12$

> Remember what 'divide' means. It tells you how many times one number 'goes into' another number.

Revise

Sometimes we have to divide larger numbers, such as $348 \div 3$. If this is too difficult to do mentally, we can use a written method. Look at how we write this down.

$$\begin{array}{r} 1\ \ 1\ \ 6 \\ 3\ \overline{)\ 3\ \ 4\ \ {}^1 8} \end{array}$$

- To begin, we divide 3 into the 3. This goes once so we write 1 above the 3.
- Then we look at the 4. 3 goes into 4 once with one remaining. So we put 1 above the 4 and carry the remaining 1 to the 8 to make 18.
- 3 goes into 18 six times, so we write 6 above 18.
- So, 348 divided by 3 equals 116.

> Check it with a multiplication! $3 \times 116 = 348$

💡 Tips

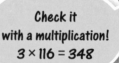

- Sometimes you might not be able to divide into the first number, so you need to carry it to the next number.

$$\begin{array}{r} 0\ \ 4\ \ 2 \\ 3\ \overline{)\ 1\ \ {}^1 2\ \ 6} \end{array}$$

💬 Talk maths

Look at the short division below and explain it aloud, saying how each stage was done.

```
    1  3  5
5 | 6 ¹7 ²5
```

✔ Check

1. Complete each of these short divisions.

a.
| 5 | 1 | 2 | 5 |

b.
| 3 | 7 | 2 |

c.
| 5 | 9 | 0 |

d.
| 4 | 5 | 3 | 2 |

e.
| 2 | 2 | 3 | 3 | 4 |

f.
| 7 | 7 | 4 | 9 |

2. Use a written method for short division.

   a. 116 ÷ 2
   b. 215 ÷ 5
   c. 426 ÷ 3
   d. 616 ÷ 4
   e. 372 ÷ 6
   f. 927 ÷ 9

⚠ Problems

Brain-teaser There are 628 children in Pigwarts School. They are divided equally into four different House Teams.

How many children are there in each House? _____

Brain-buster Jen and her mum are going on a Swimathon. They have to swim 2760 metres in 5 hours. How many metres will they swim each hour if they swim at a steady pace?

_____ metres each hour

Equivalent fractions

↺ Recap

A fraction of a whole is an amount less than 1. It shows the whole divided into **equal** parts.

Two halves make a whole.

Three thirds make a whole.

Four quarters make a whole.

Six sixths make a whole.

Two quarters is equivalent to one half. We say that $\frac{2}{4}$ and $\frac{1}{2}$ are equivalent fractions. They represent the same amount.

Two sixths is equivalent to one third. We say that $\frac{2}{6}$ and $\frac{1}{3}$ are equivalent fractions. They represent the same amount.

目 Revise

We can use diagrams to show equivalent fractions, such as fraction walls.

1 whole									
$\frac{1}{5}$		$\frac{1}{5}$		$\frac{1}{5}$		$\frac{1}{5}$		$\frac{1}{5}$	
$\frac{1}{10}$	$\frac{1}{10}$	$\frac{1}{10}$	$\frac{1}{10}$	$\frac{1}{10}$	$\frac{1}{10}$	$\frac{1}{10}$	$\frac{1}{10}$	$\frac{1}{10}$	$\frac{1}{10}$

Five fifths make a whole.
Ten tenths make a whole.

The wall shows us that two tenths is equivalent to one fifth, four tenths are equivalent to two fifths, and so on.

💡 Tips

This makes it much easier to spot equivalent fractions!

- Remember: when you divide a shape into fractions, every part must be the same size.

Talk maths

Working with a partner, use counters or paper to cover up fractions in the fraction wall. Then say what fraction has been covered and what its equivalents are.

1							
$\frac{1}{2}$				$\frac{1}{2}$			
$\frac{1}{4}$		$\frac{1}{4}$		$\frac{1}{4}$		$\frac{1}{4}$	
$\frac{1}{8}$	$\frac{1}{8}$	$\frac{1}{8}$	$\frac{1}{8}$	$\frac{1}{8}$	$\frac{1}{8}$	$\frac{1}{8}$	$\frac{1}{8}$

Try making your own fraction wall, with one whole, thirds, sixths and ninths.

Two quarters is equivalent to one half.

Six eighths is equivalent to three quarters.

✔ Check

1. Shade each circle to show the fraction.

   a. $\frac{1}{3}$ b. $\frac{3}{4}$

   c. $\frac{2}{5}$ d. $\frac{3}{4}$

2. Draw a line to join each fraction in the top row to its equivalent below.

   $\frac{1}{2}$ $\frac{1}{3}$ $\frac{1}{4}$ $\frac{1}{6}$

   $\frac{3}{12}$ $\frac{2}{12}$ $\frac{4}{12}$ $\frac{6}{12}$

3. Circle the correct equivalent fraction.

   a. $\frac{3}{4}$: $\frac{5}{8}$ $\frac{6}{8}$ $\frac{7}{8}$ $\frac{8}{8}$

   b. $\frac{2}{3}$: $\frac{8}{9}$ $\frac{7}{9}$ $\frac{6}{9}$ $\frac{5}{9}$

   c. $\frac{5}{8}$: $\frac{8}{16}$ $\frac{9}{16}$ $\frac{10}{16}$ $\frac{11}{16}$

   d. $\frac{3}{5}$: $\frac{8}{20}$ $\frac{10}{20}$ $\frac{12}{20}$ $\frac{14}{20}$

⚠ Problems

Brain-teaser Jane is racing against Paul. Jane has finished $\frac{3}{4}$ of the race and Paul has finished $\frac{5}{8}$.

Who is nearer to the finish?

_____

Brain-buster Tina is racing against Joe. Tina has finished $\frac{7}{10}$ of the race and Joe has finished $\frac{4}{5}$.

Who is nearer to the finish?

_____

Adding and subtracting fractions

↻ Recap

$\frac{1}{10}$	$\frac{1}{10}$	$\frac{1}{10}$	$\frac{1}{10}$	$\frac{1}{10}$	$\frac{1}{10}$	$\frac{1}{10}$	$\frac{1}{10}$	$\frac{1}{10}$	$\frac{1}{10}$

$$\frac{7}{10} + \frac{3}{10} = \frac{10}{10}$$

$\frac{1}{7}$	$\frac{1}{7}$	$\frac{1}{7}$	$\frac{1}{7}$			

$$\frac{1}{7} + \frac{3}{7} = \frac{4}{7}$$

$\frac{1}{5}$	$\frac{1}{5}$	$\frac{1}{5}$	$\frac{1}{5}$	$\frac{1}{5}$

$$\frac{5}{5} - \frac{4}{5} = \frac{1}{5}$$

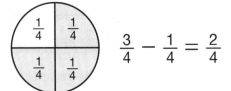 $\frac{3}{4} - \frac{1}{4} = \frac{2}{4}$

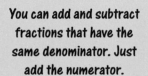

You can add and subtract fractions that have the same denominator. Just add the numerator.

📋 Revise

Improper fractions have a numerator bigger than their denominator.

We can still add and subtract improper fractions, but you must still only add and subtract the numerators.

$\frac{5}{2} + \frac{6}{2} = \frac{11}{2}$ Five halves plus six halves equals eleven halves.

$\frac{3}{4} + \frac{5}{4} = \frac{8}{4}$ Three quarters plus five quarters equals eight quarters.

$\frac{7}{3} - \frac{5}{3} = \frac{2}{3}$ Seven thirds minus five thirds equals two thirds.

$\frac{9}{6} - \frac{4}{6} = \frac{5}{6}$ Nine sixths minus four sixths equals five sixths.

💡 Tips

- You can add three or more fractions, just like you can add three or more whole numbers. $\frac{2}{3} + \frac{4}{3} + \frac{5}{3} + \frac{3}{3} = \frac{14}{3}$

💬 Talk maths

You can practise subtraction too: 'one whole minus three quarters'.

Remember:

A whole always has the same denominator and numerator.

$\frac{7}{7}$ = 1 whole $\frac{3}{3}$ = 1 whole $\frac{625}{625}$ = 1 whole

Challenge a partner to find the rest of the whole.

For example, if you say 'six eighths', they must reply 'plus two eighths makes a whole'. If you say 'seven twelfths', your partner must say 'plus five twelfths makes a whole'.

Try it with larger fractions. 'Nine twentieths' ... 'plus eleven twentieths makes a whole' and so on.

✔ Check

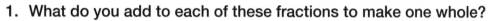

1. **What do you add to each of these fractions to make one whole?**

   a. $\frac{1}{2}$ + _____ = 1   **b.** $\frac{3}{4}$ + _____ = 1   **c.** $\frac{1}{3}$ + _____ = 1   **d.** $\frac{3}{7}$ + _____ = 1

2. **Complete these subtractions from one whole.**

   a. $1 - \frac{1}{2}$ = _____   **b.** $1 - \frac{2}{5}$ = _____   **c.** $1 - \frac{7}{8}$ = _____   **d.** $1 - \frac{13}{20}$ = _____

3. **Add these fractions.**

   a. $\frac{3}{4} + \frac{2}{4}$ = _____   **b.** $\frac{4}{5} + \frac{3}{5}$ = _____   **c.** $\frac{6}{10} + \frac{3}{10}$ = _____

   d. $\frac{5}{8} + \frac{6}{8}$ = _____   **e.** $\frac{2}{7} + \frac{4}{7} + \frac{5}{7}$ = _____   **f.** $\frac{5}{6} + \frac{4}{6} + \frac{3}{6}$ = _____

4. **Subtract these fractions.**

   a. $\frac{5}{3} - \frac{1}{3}$ = _____   **b.** $\frac{5}{6} - \frac{2}{6}$ = _____   **c.** $\frac{13}{8} - \frac{7}{8}$ = _____

   d. $\frac{7}{4} - \frac{1}{4}$ = _____   **e.** $\frac{4}{5} - \frac{1}{5}$ = _____   **f.** $\frac{21}{20} - \frac{8}{20}$ = _____

⚠ Problems

Brain-teaser A pizza is cut into 12 equal slices. Tina eats half of it, Josie eats $\frac{2}{12}$ and Dan eats $\frac{3}{12}$.

What fraction of the pizza is left? _____

Brain-buster Some children share a bucket of popcorn. Tom takes $\frac{3}{20}$ and Amanda takes $\frac{6}{20}$.

What fraction of the popcorn is left? _____

Tenths and hundredths

↻ Recap

And there are 100 hundredths in a whole!

There are ten tenths in a whole.

$\frac{1}{10}$	$\frac{1}{10}$	$\frac{1}{10}$	$\frac{1}{10}$	$\frac{1}{10}$	$\frac{1}{10}$	$\frac{1}{10}$	$\frac{1}{10}$	$\frac{1}{10}$	$\frac{1}{10}$

📝 Revise

We get tenths when we divide an object or number by 10.

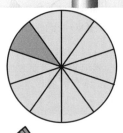

One pizza is divided between 10 people.
Each person will receive $\frac{1}{10}$ of a pizza.

Now imagine if $\frac{1}{10}$ of the pizza was shared between 10 other people.

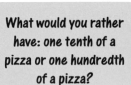

$\frac{1}{10}$ divided by 10 will give each person $\frac{1}{100}$ of the pizza. Not much!

We can count in tenths and hundredths.

What would you rather have: one tenth of a pizza or one hundredth of a pizza?

Ten hundredths equal one tenth.

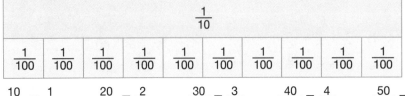

$\frac{10}{100} = \frac{1}{10}$ $\frac{20}{100} = \frac{2}{10}$ $\frac{30}{100} = \frac{3}{10}$ $\frac{40}{100} = \frac{4}{10}$ $\frac{50}{100} = \frac{5}{10}$

$\frac{60}{100} = \frac{6}{10}$ $\frac{70}{100} = \frac{7}{10}$ $\frac{80}{100} = \frac{8}{10}$ $\frac{90}{100} = \frac{9}{10}$ $\frac{100}{100} = \frac{10}{10}$

💡 Tips

- Remember $\frac{50}{100}$ is equivalent to $\frac{5}{10}$, and both are the same amount as $\frac{1}{2}$.
- $1 \div 10 = \frac{1}{10}$ = one tenth

  $1 \div 100 = \frac{1}{100}$ = one hundredth

Talk maths

Seven tenths.

Eight tenths, nine tenths, ten tenths, eleven tenths…

Play *Beat the clock*.

Working with a partner, take turns to say any fraction in tenths or hundredths, such as two tenths or seventeen hundredths. Your partner then has to count on 10 more tenths or hundredths in less than 30 seconds.

✔ Check

1. **Add these tenths and hundredths.**

   a. $\frac{1}{10} + \frac{6}{10} =$ _____
   b. $\frac{7}{10} + \frac{5}{10} =$ _____
   c. $\frac{13}{10} + \frac{9}{10} =$ _____
   d. $\frac{31}{100} + \frac{7}{100} =$ _____
   e. $\frac{78}{100} + \frac{3}{100} =$ _____
   f. $\frac{120}{100} + \frac{60}{100} =$ _____

2. **Subtract these tenths and hundredths.**

   a. $\frac{9}{10} - \frac{4}{10} =$ _____
   b. $\frac{7}{10} - \frac{5}{10} =$ _____
   c. $\frac{23}{10} - \frac{9}{10} =$ _____
   d. $\frac{21}{100} - \frac{11}{100} =$ _____
   e. $\frac{58}{100} - \frac{6}{100} =$ _____
   f. $\frac{125}{100} - \frac{80}{100} =$ _____

3. **Write these fractions in words.**

   a. $\frac{6}{10}$ _____
   b. $\frac{9}{10}$ _____
   c. $\frac{14}{100}$ _____
   d. $\frac{91}{100}$ _____

4. **Write these as fractions.**

   a. seven tenths _____
   b. thirteen tenths _____
   c. thirty-five hundredths _____
   d. two hundredths _____

⚠ Problems

Brain-teaser Complete this sentence.

Three tenths = ☐ hundredths

Brain-buster Complete this sentence.

Sixty-three hundredths = ☐ tenths and ☐ hundredths

Fraction and decimal equivalents

↺ Recap

A fraction is a proportion of one whole.

$\frac{1}{100}$ $\frac{1}{10}$ $\frac{1}{4}$ $\frac{1}{2}$ $\frac{3}{4}$ are all fractions.

Revise

100s	10s	1s	0.1s	0.01s
			.	

Numbers less than one can also be represented by decimals.

To show tenths and hundredths using our number system, we use a decimal point and two new columns.

- We write three tenths as 0.3 and five hundredths as 0.05.
- We can say that the number 0.47 has four tenths and seven hundredths.
- We read decimals aloud, using digits zero to nine.
- Any fraction can be written as a decimal.

Fraction	$\frac{1}{2}$	$\frac{1}{4}$	$\frac{3}{4}$	$\frac{1}{10}$	$\frac{4}{10}$	$\frac{61}{100}$	$\frac{73}{100}$
Decimal	0.5	0.25	0.75	0.1	0.4	0.61	0.73

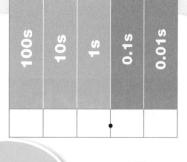

We say 0.5 is 'zero point five'.

We say 0.75 is 'zero point seven five'.

We can also have whole numbers and decimals.

For 23.62 we would say twenty-three, six tenths and two hundredths.

Or twenty-three point six two.

💡 Tips

- Decimals with **one decimal place** are equivalent to a fraction with a denominator of 10.

  $0.6 = \frac{6}{10}$

- Decimals with **two decimal places** are equivalent to a fraction with a denominator of 100.

  $0.37 = \frac{37}{100}$

  0.1 is one tenth ($\frac{1}{10}$)

  0.2 is two tenths ($\frac{2}{10}$)

  0.3 is three tenths ($\frac{3}{10}$)

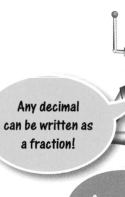

Any decimal can be written as a fraction!

Can you keep going?

💬 Talk maths

'Three tenths' or 'zero point three'.

Practise saying these decimals both ways.

0.3	0.17	0.4	0.08	0.85
0.75	0.2	0.02	0.31	0.11
	0.1			
0.05	0.43	3.14	0.66	0.99

'One tenth and seven hundredths' or 'zero point one seven'.

✔ Check

1. Write the shaded part of each whole as a decimal.

   a. 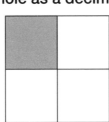 _____

   b. 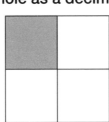 _____

   c. 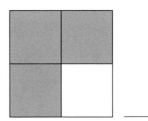 _____

2. Change these fractions to their decimal equivalents.

   a. $\frac{1}{2}$ = _____

   b. $\frac{3}{4}$ = _____

   c. $\frac{1}{10}$ = _____

   d. $\frac{27}{100}$ = _____

   e. $\frac{1}{4}$ = _____

   f. $\frac{8}{10}$ = _____

3. Change these decimals to their fraction equivalents.

   a. 0.25 = _____

   b. 0.78 = _____

   c. 0.4 = _____

   d. 0.75 = _____

   e. 0.5 = _____

   f. 0.21 = _____

⚠ Problems

Brain-teaser Tim says that zero point two is the same as $\frac{2}{10}$.

Explain why he is right. _____

Brain-buster Zoe says that seventy-five hundredths is the same as three quarters.

Explain if she is wrong or right. _____

Working with decimals

↻ Recap

Our number system uses **place value**.

We sometimes call this 100s, 10s and 1s.
346 is three hundred and forty-six.
Between zero and one we use decimal fractions.
.12 is point one two.

100s	10s	1s	0.1s	0.01s
3	4	6 •	1	2

Decimals show tenths and hundredths of a whole.
These are sometimes called decimal fractions.

DID YOU KNOW?

When you solve money problems with pounds and pence, you often use decimals.

📝 Revise

There are lots of ways we can work with decimals.

Dividing whole numbers by 10 or 100

We move the place value one column to the right when dividing by 10.
$\frac{3}{10} = 3 \div 10 = 0.3$

We move the place value two columns to the right when dividing by 100.
$\frac{45}{100} = 45 \div 100 = 0.45$

Look at these examples: $\frac{7}{10} = 0.7$ and $\frac{7}{100} = 0.07$
$\frac{23}{10} = 2.3$ and $\frac{23}{100} = 0.23$

Rounding decimals just like other numbers

Rounding to the nearest whole number: $0.7 \rightarrow 1$ $4.2 \rightarrow 4$ $6.8 \rightarrow 7$ $3.5 \rightarrow 4$

If it is .5 or higher, round up. If it is lower than .5, round down.

Ordering and comparing decimals

0.8 is bigger than 0.5 (eight tenths is bigger than 5 tenths).

0.25 is smaller than 0.32 (thirty-two hundredths is bigger than twenty-five hundredths).

💡 Tips

We can draw number lines for decimals too!

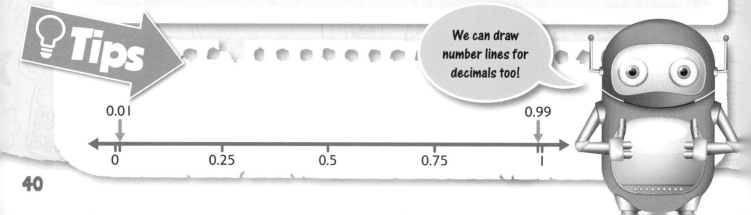

0.01

0.99

0   0.25   0.5   0.75   1

Talk maths

Choose ten numbers between 10 and 100, like the ones in the box below.
Take any two of the numbers and divide each one by 100.
Next, make a true statement about your numbers.

12	19	23	37	42	69
53		84	95	75	

For example: 23 and 75
$23 \div 100 = 0.23$ $75 \div 100 = 0.75$

0.23 is less than 0.75. 0.75 is greater than 0.23.

You can extend this activity by writing each decimal on a number line from 0 to 1.

✔ Check

1. Complete these divisions.

   a. $7 \div 10 =$ _____   b. $31 \div 100 =$ _____   c. $3 \div 10 =$ _____   d. $94 \div 100 =$ _____

2. Round these decimals to the nearest whole number.

   a. $4.8 =$ _____   b. $3.1 =$ _____   c. $5.5 =$ _____   d. $7.4 =$ _____

3. Insert the correct signs. Use <, > or =.

   a. 0.7 _____ 0.75   b. 0.31 _____ 0.42   c. 0.6 _____ 0.60   d. 0.25 _____ 0.23

4. Position these decimals on the number line.

   0.5   0.9   0.05   0.75   0.65   0.25   0.35

   0 ————————————————————————————————— 1

⚠ Problems

Brain-teaser Brenda knows that 65 divided by 100 = 0.65.

What would 65 divided by 10 be? _____

Brain-buster Thomas says that 0.55 rounded to the nearest whole number is 1.

What would 0.55 rounded to the nearest tenth be? _____

Units of measurement

↺ Recap

Different quantities are measured in different ways.

Quantity	Units of measurement	Abbreviations	
Time (years)	1 year = 12 months 1 week = 7 days	years = y months = m	weeks = w days = d
Time (days)	1 day = 24 hours 1 hour = 60 minutes 1 minute = 60 seconds	hours = h minutes = m	seconds = s
Money	1 pound = 100 pence	pounds = £	pence = p
Mass	1 kilogram = 1000 grams	kilograms = kg	grams = g
Capacity	1 litre = 1000 millilitres	litre = l	millilitre = ml
Length	1 kilometre = 1000 metres 1 metre = 100 centimetres 1 centimetre = 10 millimetres	kilometres = km centimetres = cm millimetres = mm	metres = m

📄 Revise

Think about where you see the different units above, and what they are used for.

Quantity	How to measure	Why	Examples
Time (years)	calendars, clocks	planning years, days	holidays, timetables
Money	notes and coins	buying and selling	school meals
Mass	scales and weights	to know correct amounts	making cakes
Capacity	containers	to know correct amounts	mixing drinks
Length	rulers, tape measures, maps	making things, planning journeys	making a box, going on a trip

💡 Tips

- How far do you walk to school?
- How many days have you been alive?
- Do you have a water bottle? What is its capacity?
- Guess the weight of your dinner. How can you check?
- How much pocket money do you receive each year?

Talk maths

Play *Read my mind*.
Take turns with a partner to give clues about the units you are thinking about. Try thinking of different clues for all the units on the opposite page.

Can you think of more challenging clues?

Example clue	Answer
a cup of tea	millilitres
a long journey	kilometres
a finger	centimetres
a snail	grams
a new car	pounds
a maths lesson	minutes
a cricket match	hours
a lifetime	years

✔ Check

1. **What units would you measure these things in?**

   a. The length of a pencil _____   b. The height of a house _____

   c. The cost of a pencil _____   d. The cost of a car _____

   e. The capacity of a cup _____   f. The capacity of a bath _____

   g. The weight of a computer _____   h. The weight of a pencil _____

   i. The duration of pop song _____   j. The duration of a holiday _____

2. **Write the names of this measuring equipment.**

   a.    b.   c.

   _____   _____   _____

3. **What equipment would you use to measure these items?**

   a. The length of a pencil _____   b. The height of your teacher _____

   c. The capacity of a cup _____   d. The weight of an apple _____

   e. A running race _____   f. The time until Christmas _____

⚠ Problems

Brain-teaser 1 millilitre of water weighs 1 gram.
How much does 5 litres of water weigh, in grams? _____

Brain-buster Tyler's dad is one metre seventy-three centimetres tall.
Tyler is exactly half the height of his dad. How tall is Tyler in millimetres? _____

Units of time

↻ Recap

These are all units of time: seconds, minutes, hours, days, weeks and years.

60 seconds = 1 minute
60 minutes = 1 hour
24 hours = 1 day
7 days = 1 week
365 days = 1 year

Remember that months are not all the same length.
30 days hath September, April, June and November.
All the rest have 31, except for February all alone.
(February has 28 days, and 29 days in a leap year.)

Also, we say that there are 52 weeks in a year, but this is not exactly true, it is an approximation. Look: 7 × 52 = 364 days

📄 Revise

To convert between times is tricky!

Convert	Calculation	Example
years to months	× 12	3 years = 3 × 12 = 36 months
years to days	× 365	2 years = 2 × 365 = 730 days
weeks to days	× 7	6 weeks = 6 × 7 = 42 days
days to hours	× 24	3 days = 3 × 24 = 72 hours
hours to minutes	× 60	5 hours = 5 × 60 = 300 minutes
minutes to seconds	× 60	10 minutes = 10 × 60 = 600 seconds

💡 Tips

- 1 year = 365 days × 24 hours × 60 minutes × 60 seconds!

If you want to convert from a large unit, such as years, to a small unit such as seconds, you have to do one stage at a time.

 **Talk maths**

Work with an adult and think about how long different things take to do in seconds.

Task	Time	In seconds
putting on shoes	2 minutes	120 seconds
walking to school	$5\frac{1}{2}$ minutes	330 seconds

 **Check**

1. **Draw lines to match the time in the top row to its equivalent on the bottom row.**

   2 years   2 weeks   2 days   2 hours   2 minutes

   120 minutes   730 days   120 seconds   48 hours   14 days

2. **Convert each of these times.**

   a. 2 minutes = _____ seconds

   b. 3 hours = _____ minutes

   c. 4 days = _____ hours

   d. 5 weeks = _____ days

   e. 6 years = _____ months

   f. 2 years (not leap years) = _____ days

3. **Convert each of these times.**

   a. $3\frac{1}{2}$ minutes = _____ seconds

   b. $2\frac{1}{2}$ hours = _____ minutes

   c. $5\frac{1}{2}$ days = _____ hours

   d. $7\frac{1}{2}$ years = _____ months

⚠ **Problems**

Brain-teaser Poppy knows that on her tenth birthday she will have lived for three leap years and seven ordinary years.

How many days has she lived altogether? _____

Brain-buster a. How many hours are there in a non-leap year? _____

 b. How many minutes are there in a day? _____

Analogue and digital clocks

↻ Recap

When we use the 12-hour clock, we divide the day into two halves of 12 hours each, from midnight to noon, and then back to midnight.

For 12-hour clock time, we have to say am or pm.

24-hour clocks are different – they do just what they say. They start at midnight and count 24 hours through the day.

This is an analogue clock.
It uses hands to show the time.
It is a 12-hour clock.
It shows twenty-three minutes past ten, but is it am or pm?

> am and pm are 'before noon' and 'after noon' to you and me!

> You have to look out the window and see if it is day or night!

🗒 Revise

Digital clocks use digits to show hours and minutes.

For 12-hour digital times, we have to use am and pm. This shows that the time is before noon or after noon.

Converting between 12-hour and 24-hour digital times isn't so hard.

For pm times, we add 12 to get the 24-hour time for example, 10:15pm = 22:15pm.

For 24-hour times past 12 noon, just subtract 12 to get the 12-hour time, for example 16:47 = 4:47pm.

> 11:35pm = 23:35
> 6:42pm = 18:42

> 13:25 = 1:25pm
> 22:45 = 10:45pm

💡 Tips

> Learn how to convert between analogue and digital.

- 'Past' times are easy. We just write the hours and the number of minutes. For example, 10:05 is five minutes past 10.

- 'To' times are harder. Learn that 30 is half past, 40 is twenty to, 45 is quarter to and 50 is ten to.

💬 Talk maths

Work with a partner to become an expert time-teller.

Draw an analogue clock like this. Put hands on the clock, using a long pencil and a short pencil, and say am or pm. Then challenge your partner to say this in 12-hour or 24-hour digital time.

Then write digital clock times, such as 17:35. Ask your partner to show you the time on the analogue clock.

✔ Check

1. Complete this chart for 12-hour analogue and digital times.

Analogue	twelve noon		ten past eleven	five to four	
Digital		8:45			3:15

2. Write these analogue times as 24-hour digital times.

a. am   b. pm   c. am   d. pm

_____   _____   _____   _____

3. Write these 24-hour digital times as 12-hour analogue times.

a.    b.    c.    d.

_____   _____   _____   _____

⚠ Problems

Brain-teaser A train departs at quarter to eleven in the morning and arrives at 12:05pm.

How long does the journey take? _____

Brain-buster An aeroplane takes off from London at 21:45 and flies directly to South Africa. The aeroplane lands at 9:25am London time.

How long was the flight? _____

47

Money

↻ Recap

These are the coins we use in England and Wales.
We also use £5, £10, £20 and £50 notes.

📄 Revise

Money shows us the cost of things.
We use pounds and pence.
£1 = 100 pence

We show pence using two decimal places.

7 pounds and 25 pence = £7.25

That's *seven pounds twenty-five*.

Unlike other decimals, if the last digit is a zero, we still write it in.

16 pounds and 50 pence = £16.50
That's *sixteen pounds fifty*.

Look at this amount: £0.59 is zero pounds and fifty-nine pence, or 59p

To convert pounds to pence, multiply by 100:
£6.50 = 6.50 × 100 = 650p

To convert pence to pounds divide by 100:
3265p = 3265 ÷ 100 = £32.65

DID YOU KNOW?

Before the year 1971 we used pounds, shillings and pence. A shilling was worth 12 old pennies and there were 240 old pennies in a pound!

1p is one hundredth of one pound.

Notice that if you use the £ sign and decimals, you don't add a p at the end.

💡 Tips

Operation	Example
Addition	£3.50 + £2.15 = £5.65
Subtraction	£5.00 − £1.25 = £3.75
Multiplication	£2.10 × 3 = £6.30
Division	£7.00 ÷ 2 = £3.50
Fractions	$\frac{1}{2}$ of £25.00 = £12.50

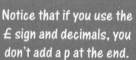

You can use all your number skills to solve money problems.

- We can use written methods with money just like any other numbers.
- Remember to be careful with the decimal point.

💬 Talk maths

I'd like a tin of beans for 32p. Here is £1.

Here is your change: 68p.

Find an old shopping receipt or a price list from a catalogue or website, and work with a partner to compare costs.

Next, challenge each other by asking for items on the list and paying for them.

If you feel confident, put the money away and solve problems just using the maths.

✔ Check

1. Convert these pence to pounds.

Pence	500p	150p	3300p	59p	1000p
Pounds					

2. Convert these pounds to pence.

Pounds	£1	£4.25	£0.62	£20	£12.06
Pence					

3. Complete these calculations.

a. £2.50 + £3.30 = _____

b. £4.90 + £3.20 = _____

c. £10.00 − £6.50 = _____

d. £20.00 − £12.99 = _____

e. 8 × 50p = £ _____

f. £2.50 × 4 = £ _____

g. £20 ÷ 4 = £ _____

h. £15 ÷ 3 = £ _____

⚠ Problems

Brain-teaser Ice creams cost £1.25 each. Alfie's mum buys five.

a. What is the total cost? _____

b. How much change will she get from a £10 note? _____

Brain-buster Ice creams cost £1.25 each and ice lollies cost £1.50 each.

a. How much would three ice creams and seven lollies cost altogether? _____

b. How much change would there be from a £20 note? _____

Mass and capacity

DID YOU KNOW?

1 litre of water weighs 1 kilogram.
So, 1 millilitre of water weighs 1 gram.

↻ Recap

Mass tells us the weight of things.

We measure mass in grams and kilograms.
1000g = 1kg

Capacity tells us how much a container can hold.

We measure capacity in millilitres and litres.
1000ml = 1l

📋 Revise

To add masses, each mass must be in kilograms, or in grams.

The units must be the same.

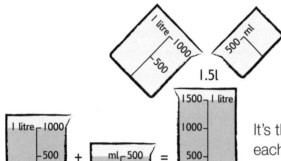

1.5l

It's the same with capacity: to add or subtract capacities, each capacity must be in litres, or in millilitres.

The units must be the same.

💡 Tips

These charts may be useful for converting units.

Converting mass

Kilograms	1kg	5kg	5kg 350g	$\frac{1}{4}$ kg	$\frac{1}{2}$ kg	$\frac{3}{4}$ kg
Grams	1000g	5000g	5350g	250g	500g	750g

Converting capacity

Litres	1l	3l	4l 825ml	$\frac{1}{4}$ l	$\frac{1}{2}$ l	$\frac{3}{4}$ l
Millilitres	1000ml	3000ml	4825ml	250ml	500ml	750ml

Talk maths

Working with an adult, look in the kitchen cupboards or visit a shop. Challenge each other to predict the capacity of different bottles, the mass of different bags of vegetables, and so on.

If you can, extend this work using scales and measuring jugs. Try to investigate the mass or capacity of as many different items as you can.

Remember to work safely and with adult permission at all times!

✔ Check

1. Match each capacity to the correct object.

    thimble   mug   bathtub

    200l   200ml   20ml

2. Match each mass to the correct object.

    mouse   child   elephant

    5000kg   50g   50kg

3. Convert these masses.

   a. 5kg = ___ g
   b. 6000g = ___ kg
   c. $\frac{1}{2}$kg = ___ g
   d. 4500g = ___ kg

4. Convert these capacities.

   a. 3000ml = ___ l
   b. $7\frac{1}{2}$l = ___ ml
   c. 3500ml = ___ l
   d. $\frac{1}{2}$l = ___ ml

5. Solve these calculations.

   a. $3\frac{1}{4}$kg + 500g = ___ kg
   b. 450g + 700g = ___ g
   c. $\frac{1}{10}$kg + 320g = ___ g
   d. $3\frac{1}{4}$l + 450ml = ___ ml
   e. 230ml + 140ml = ___ l
   f. $3\frac{1}{4}$l + $1\frac{3}{4}$l = ___ ml

⚠ Problems

Brain-teaser

a. A carton of juice contains 50ml. How many cartons would make 1 litre? _____

b. A pencil weighs 27g. How much would 100 pencils weigh?

_____ kilograms and _____ grams

Brain-buster

a. Paper cups have a capacity of 100ml. How many cups will a $2\frac{1}{2}$l bottle fill? _____

b. Onions weigh 125g each. How many onions would make 1 kilogram? _____

Length and distance

↺ Recap

We measure short lengths in centimetres and millimetres, and some longer lengths and distances in metres.

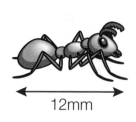

12mm

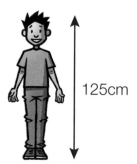

125cm

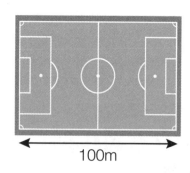

100m

Revise

We measure even longer distances in kilometres.

You should know these.   10mm = 1cm

100cm = 1m (and 1000mm = 1m)

1000m = 1km

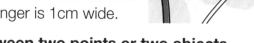

10km

A

B

Length is the measure of an object or a line from end to end.

For example, a football pitch is 100m long; a finger is 1cm wide.

Distance is the measure of the space between two points or two objects.

For example, the distance between two towns is 10km; the gap between two parked cars is 1m.

Remember tenths and hundredths?

A millimetre is one tenth of a centimetre, a centimetre is one hundredth of a metre.

💡 Tips

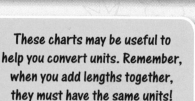

These charts may be useful to help you convert units. Remember, when you add lengths together, they must have the same units!

Millimetres	1	5	10
Centimetres	0.1	0.5	1

Centimetres	1	10	25	50	75	100
Metres	0.01	0.1	0.25	0.5	0.75	1

Metres	10	100	250	500	750	1000
Kilometres	$\frac{1}{100}$	$\frac{1}{10}$	$\frac{1}{4}$	$\frac{1}{2}$	$\frac{3}{4}$	1

💬 Talk maths

Working with a partner, challenge each other, without using a ruler, to draw a line of a particular length, or make two dots a certain distance apart.

(Never go above 12cm, but try mixtures of centimetres and millimetres, such as 5.7cm.)

Next measure the length or distance and see how accurate your partner is.

✔ Check

1. Measure the length of these lines. Give your answers in millimetres.

a. ▬▬▬▬▬▬▬ _____   b. ▬▬▬▬▬ _____

c. ▬▬▬▬▬▬ _____   d. ▬▬▬ _____

2. Measure the distances between these dots. Give your answers in centimetres.

a. A •   • B _____

b. A •   • B _____

c. A •   • B _____

3. Complete these conversion charts.

a.

mm	cm
10	
100	
	2
35	
	100

b.

cm	m
100	
1000	
	0.25
	0.5
	10

c.

m	km
500	
2000	
	$\frac{1}{4}$
	1
	9

⚠ Problems

Brain-teaser Ahmed is 1.52m tall. He wears shoes with a 2cm heel.

What height will he be with his shoes on? _____m or _____cm

Brain-buster The distance between two towns is 19km. Isobel is going to ride her bike between the towns, and wants to stop halfway. How far will she ride for each half of the journey?

Give your answer in km and in m: _____km or _____m

53

Perimeter

↺ Recap

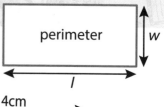

Perimeter is the distance around the sides of a shape.

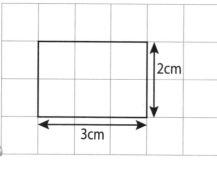

This rectangle has a perimeter of 3 + 3 + 2 + 2 = 10cm.

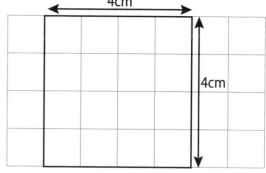

This square has a perimeter of 4 + 4 + 4 + 4 = 16cm.

📄 Revise

If we say that all rectangles have a length *l* and a width *w*, then the perimeter can be calculated with a formula.

We can say $P = l + w + l + w$

Or, changing the order that we add in: $P = l + l + w + w$

We can make this simpler too: $P = 2l + 2w$

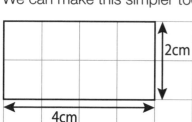

The perimeter of this rectangle is
$P = 2 \times 4 + 2 \times 2 = 12$cm

What do you think the perimeter of a rectangle 6m long and 3m wide would be?

💡 Tips

Here's a quick way to find the perimeter of a square.

- The formula for a square is easier, because all the sides are the same length.

  $P = 4s$

- $P = 4 \times 3 = 12$cm

💬 Talk maths

Use a pencil and a ruler to draw a selection of rectangles and squares, each with different measurements. Label your shapes A, B, C and write the lengths of the sides separately.

Next, challenge someone you know to estimate the perimeter of each shape. Use a ruler to check their estimates. How many can they get right?

✔ Check

1. **Draw each of these shapes and then write their perimeter inside them.**

   a. A rectangle, length 4cm, width 2cm.

   b. A square, side length 3cm.

2. **Calculate the perimeter of these shapes.**

   a.

   b.

   c.

3. **Complete this chart.**

Shape	Length	Width	Perimeter
rectangle	5cm	2cm	
rectangle	12mm	5mm	
rectangle	6km	2km	
square	8mm	8mm	
square	5m	5m	
square	4.5cm	4.5cm	

⚠ Problems

Brain-teaser A square field is $3\frac{1}{2}$ km long on each side.

How long is the fence that goes around it? _____

55

Area

↻ Recap

A 2D shape is flat. 2D means two-dimensional.

We can accurately draw 2D shapes on paper with a pencil and a ruler.

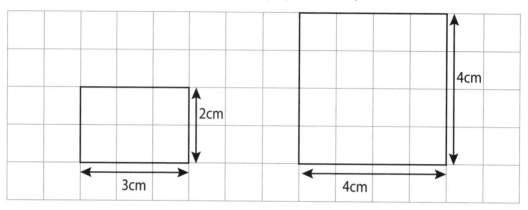

Remember, a rectangle has right angles at each corner, and the opposite sides are the same length.

A square is a type of rectangle, where all sides are the same length.

📝 Revise

Area is measured in squares.

This square is 1 square long and 1 square high. We say its area is 1 square.

We can simply count squares to calculate simple areas.

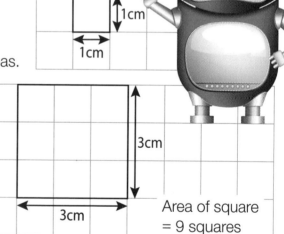

Area of rectangle = 8 squares

Area of square = 9 squares

💡 Tips

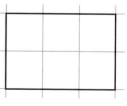

- This shape is 2 squares wide and 3 squares long. It looks like an array that we use in multiplication. We could write 2 × 3 for the array. We can use this multiplication fact to work out the area.

There are 2 lots of 3 squares. **So the area is 6 squares.**

Talk maths

Some of these have more than one answer. Can you find them all?

Work with a partner to draw each of these shapes, if possible on squared paper.

Before you start discuss what you think the length and height of each shape will be.

Shape	rectangle	rectangle	rectangle	square	square	square
Area	6 squares	8 squares	12 squares	1 square	4 squares	16 squares
Length						
Width						

✔ Check

1. Count squares to find the area of each shape.

a.   b.   c.

d.

2. Find the area of these shapes. You can draw them on squared paper to help you.

a. A rectangle that is 4 squares long and 3 squares high: _____

b. A square that is 3 squares long and 3 squares high: _____

⚠ Problems

Brain-teaser Sanjay draws a rectangle 12 squares long and 7 squares high, and a square with each side 8 squares long. Which shape has the greater area, and by how much?

_____

Brain-buster Mark makes a wall from wooden blocks. It is 3 blocks high and 4 blocks long. It has a gap that is 1 block wide and 2 blocks high.

How many blocks does Mark use for his wall? _____

Angles

↻ Recap

Angles are used to measure how much things turn.

- A quarter of a turn is called a right angle.
- A half-turn is two right angles.
- Three quarters of a turn is three right angles.
- There are four right angles in a complete turn.

Angles are also used to measure the gap where two straight lines meet.

Revise

Acute: less than a right angle

Right angle:

Obtuse: more than a right angle, less than two right angles

✔ Check

1. What is each angle: an acute angle, an obtuse angle, or a right angle?

a.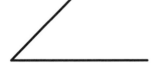

b.

c.

_____   _____   _____

2. Number these angles a, b, c and d, going from smallest to largest.

a.

b.

c.

d.

_____   _____   _____   _____

⚠ Problems

Brain-teaser Draw a triangle and cut it out. Cut off each angle.
Put them together so that the points are touching. What do you notice? _____

Triangles

⟳ Recap

A triangle is a 2D shape with three straight sides. It also has three angles.

- Angles less than a quarter turn are called **acute**.
- A **right angle** is a quarter turn.
- Angles between one and two right angles are called **obtuse**.

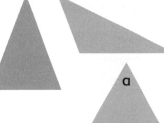

Tri means three, so triangle means three angles!

📄 Revise

There are several types of triangle.

Equilateral	Isosceles	Right-angled	Scalene

All sides are the same length. All angles are the same size.	Two sides are the same length. Two angles are the same.	One angle is a right angle.	All sides are different lengths. All angles are different sizes.

✔ Check

1. **Name each of these triangles.**

a.

b.

_____

c.

d.

_____   _____

⚠ Problems

Brain-teaser Draw one straight line to make an isosceles triangle and a scalene triangle.

59

Quadrilaterals

↻ Recap

We say that different 2D shapes have different properties.

Triangle	Square	Rectangle	Pentagon	Hexagon
3 sides	4 sides	4 sides	5 sides	6 sides

Revise

A square is a **regular** quadrilateral, and an equilateral triangle is a regular triangle. All their sides and angles are the same. **Irregular** shapes do not have equal sides or angles.

There are six types of quadrilateral.

Square	Rectangle	Rhombus	Parallelogram	Kite	Trapezium
All sides equal. All angles right angles.	Opposite sides equal. All angles right angles.	All sides equal. Opposite angles equal.	Opposite sides equal and parallel. Opposite angles equal	Adjacent sides equal.	Only one pair of parallel sides.

Adjacent means 'next to'.

Tips

Can you see the connection between a square and a rhombus?

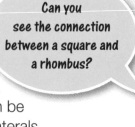

- Try making quadrilaterals with construction kits, straws or lolly sticks. You can see how they can be stretched and squashed to make other quadrilaterals.

Talk maths

Cover the names on the opposite page and practise naming each quadrilateral. Then cover the shapes and try to describe the properties for each name.

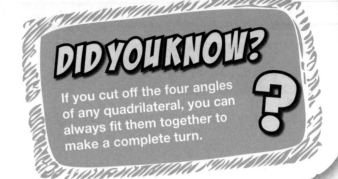

✔ Check

1. What is the difference between a square and a rectangle?

_____

2. What is the difference between a rhombus and a kite?

_____

3. What is the difference between a parallelogram and a trapezium?

_____

4. Name each quadrilateral, and then connect it to its properties.

a. _____   b. _____   c. _____   d. _____

All sides equal.
Opposite angles equal.

Adjacent sides equal.

Opposite sides equal and parallel.
Opposite angles equal.

Only one pair of parallel sides.

⚠ Problems

Brain-teaser Petra drew a quadrilateral with all sides the same length.

Which quadrilaterals could she have drawn? _____

Brain-buster Roger wants to draw a kite and thinks he can do this by joining a right-angled triangle and an isosceles triangle together. Draw a sketch to show how he could do this.

Symmetry of 2D shapes

↺ Recap

Some objects have two identical halves.

When one half is like a mirror image of the other half, we can say the object or shape is symmetrical.

📋 Revise

Look at the butterfly above. It has a **line of symmetry**. This is a bit like a mirror. One side is an identical reflection of the other.

Some objects and shapes have their lines of symmetry in different positions.

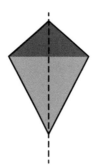   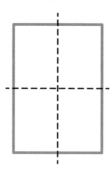

Lines of symmetry can be harder to spot. Can you see them for these two?

This diagram has two lines of symmetry.   This square has four lines of symmetry.

💡 Tips

- Remember that for patterns, colours must be symmetrical too.
- Regular shapes have the same number of lines of symmetry as they do sides.
- A circle has an infinite number of lines of symmetry.
- The letters Z and S might look symmetrical, but their halves are not mirror images.

Talk maths

With a partner, discuss these shapes and identify all the lines of symmetry. Many of them only have one line, but some have more than one.

✔ Check

1. Carefully complete these shapes to make them symmetrical.

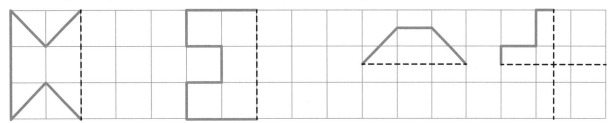

2. Draw the lines of symmetry on each number that has one or more.

1 2 3 4 5 6 7 8 9 0

3. Draw all the lines of symmetry on these regular shapes.

⚠ Problems

Brain-teaser Draw the other half of this shape to make it symmetrical.

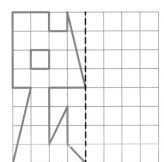

Brain-buster Tanya says she can think of four capital letters that each have two or more lines of symmetry. Can you show each letter with its lines of symmetry?

Coordinates

↺ Recap

Number lines are used for counting in equal amounts.

They can be drawn in any direction.

📋 Revise

We draw graphs with a vertical *y*-axis and a horizontal *x*-axis.
Each one is like a number line. They meet at zero.

We can plot points on the grid using coordinates. Points on the grid are always plotted with the *x*-coordinate first, and then the *y*-coordinate.

The coordinates of point G are (4, 5).

That's 4 along the x-axis, and 5 up the y-axis.

The coordinates of point H are (6, 3).

Can you find the coordinates for points J and K?

J = (____ , ____), K = (____ , ____)

We can join the points to form lines.
For the line AB, A = (3, 7), B = (8, 8)

We can also plot the corners of shapes.
Can you find the coordinates of the vertices of the triangle XYZ?

X = (____ , ____), Y = (____ , ____), Z = (____ , ____)

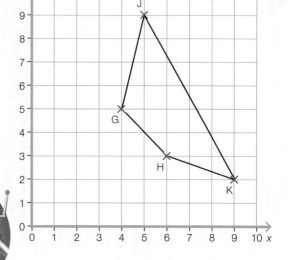

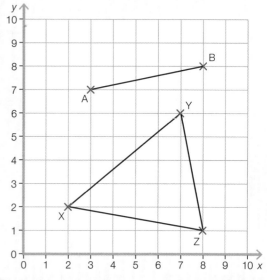

💡 Tips

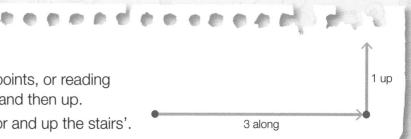

- Remember, when you are plotting points, or reading and writing coordinates, along first and then up.
- Some people say 'along the corridor and up the stairs'.

1 up

3 along

Talk maths

Challenge a partner to find the treasure at different coordinates.

Next, send them on a treasure hunt, sending them on a walk to five or six different points on the map.

The treasure is buried at (5, 4).

Start at (0, 0), next go to (6, 2), then to (3, 5)... Can your partner follow the directions?

✔ Check

1. a. Use the grid below. Write the coordinates for these points.

X = (_____ , _____), Y = (_____ , _____)

b. Plot these points.

A (2, 2)   B (2, 8)   C (8, 8)   D (8, 2)

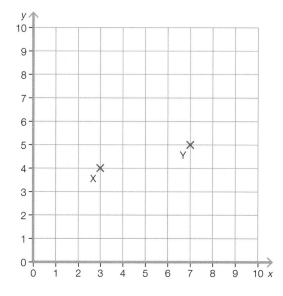

2. a. For the graph below. Write the coordinates of the triangle PQR.

P = (_____ , _____), Q = (_____ , _____),
R = (_____ , _____)

b. Draw a rectangle with vertices JKLM with these coordinates.

J (1, 1)   K (9, 1)   L (9, 7)   M (1, 7)

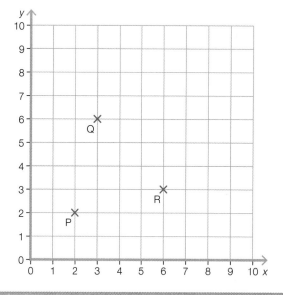

⚠ Problems

Brain-teaser Tim plots a point (7, 2). What are the coordinates of a point three squares directly above it? (_____ , _____)

Translation

↻ Recap

We draw graphs with a *y*-axis and an
x-axis.
We can join the points to form lines.
We can also plot the corners of shapes.
We write the *x*-coordinate first, then the
y-coordinate.
A = (1, 2), X = (2, 4)

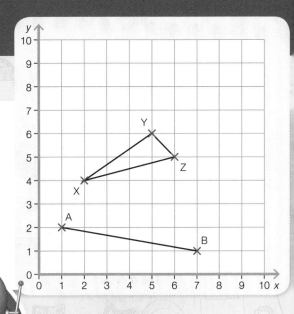

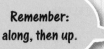

Remember:
along, then up.

Translation is when all
of the shape moves the
same distance.

📝 Revise

We can **translate** points. We can move a point on
the grid, with the *x*-coordinate and the *y*-coordinate
each moving a certain amount.

The red point A below has been translated 3 right
and 4 up. The new point has the coordinates (5, 6).

Can you see how the red points B, C and D have
been translated?

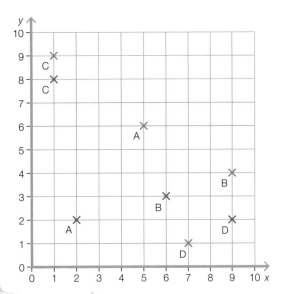

We can also translate shapes.

The square below has been translated
4 left and 3 down. Can you see how
each corner has moved the same
amount?

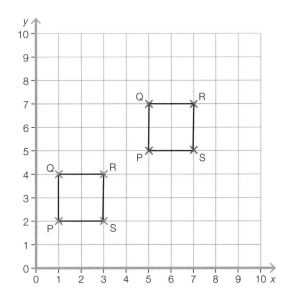

💡 Tips

- When translating a shape, all the *x*-coordinates change by the same amount, and all the
  y-coordinates do too.

Talk maths

Take turns to choose different points on a graph. Say its coordinates, and then challenge someone to translate it.

Translate (1, 1) by 2 right and 3 up.

Translate (8, 8) by 0 left and 2 down.

✔ Check

1. **a.** Using the coordinate grid below, translate the points W, X, Y and Z by 2 right and 3 down.

   b. Write the coordinates of the new points.

   W = (___, ___)   X = (___, ___)

   Y = (___, ___)   Z = (___, ___)

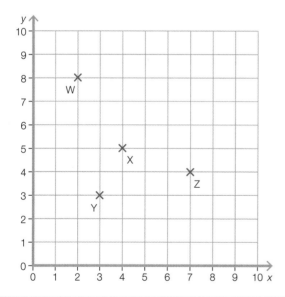

2. **Use the coordinate grid below.**

   a. Plot a triangle ABC: A (2, 2), B (4, 4), C (4, 2).

   b. Translate it 3 right and 5 up.

   c. Write the coordinates of the new shape here.

   A = (___, ___)   B = (___, ___)

   C = (___, ___)

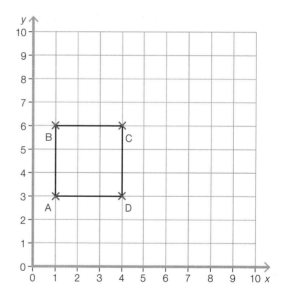

⚠ Problems

Brain-teaser Tina draws a grid and marks point X with coordinates (5, 4).

She then translates it to (0, 0). What was the translation? (_____, _____)

Tables and pictograms

↻ Recap

Pictograms provide information in an easy-to-read way. They use simple icons to represent data.

Look at this pictogram. It was created after a class survey of pets. It uses one icon for each pet counted in the survey.

Cat	☺ ☺ ☺ ☺ ☺
Dog	☺ ☺ ☺ ☺ ☺ ☺
Goldfish	
Budgie	☺ ☺ ☺
Hamster	☺ ☺ ☺

☺ = 1

- The children in this class have 17 pets altogether.
- There is the same number of budgies as hamsters.
- There are no goldfish.
- There is one more dog than cats.

📋 Revise

Complicated information is often presented in tables and charts.
This table provides information about some animals in a safari park.

Animal	Height (cm)	Weight (kg)	Average lifespan (years)	Diet
Elephant	350	5000	58	herbivore
Giraffe	530	1200	24	herbivore
Lion	100	160	17	carnivore
Rhinoceros	150	1500	45	herbivore
Zebra	130	320	23	herbivore

Notice that each column has different units.

Looking down each column we can compare the information for different animals. For example, we can say about the lion:
The lion is the only carnivore. It is the shortest animal. It is the lightest animal.

We can also do calculations. For example: *The lion is 50cm shorter than the rhinoceros.*

💡 Tips

- Use your fingers to help you read rows and columns of data. Or if you have a ruler available even better as it is easy to misread tables and charts.

Talk maths

Work with a friend to do a survey. You could do either of these.

- Create a table about your friends or families. Include information about their ages, heights, eye colour and so on.
- Create a pictogram of car colours.

When you have your data, discuss it, and ask each other questions about it.

✔ Check

1. Draw a pictogram for the weather survey below.

Use one icon for every 5 days.

Sunshine						
Rain						
Cloudy						
Snow						

Children's weather survey for a term.

Weather	Icon	Days
Sunshine	☀	10
Rain	💧	25
Cloudy	☁	30
Snow	❄	5

2. Use the animal information table on the opposite page to answer these questions.

a. Which is the heaviest animal? _____

b. Which animals are shorter than a rhinoceros? _____

c. Which two animals have a similar lifespan? _____

d. How much taller is the giraffe than the elephant? _____

e. What is the difference in weight between the rhinoceros and the giraffe? _____

f. How much longer on average does a zebra live than a lion? _____

⚠ Problems

Brain-teaser Tom thinks of two animals that are listed in the table opposite. He says one is twice as heavy as the other.

Which two animals is he thinking about? _____

Bar charts

↺ Recap

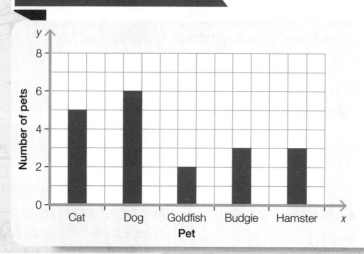

Bar charts are like pictograms in simpler form.

Instead of icons they use bars to represent the different quantities, with a scale on one axis to show the number of each item's bar.

This is a bar chart for pets in a class. Notice that the scale increases in 2s.

🗒 Revise

This is a bar chart for a car survey outside a school. The vertical axis is in 5s.

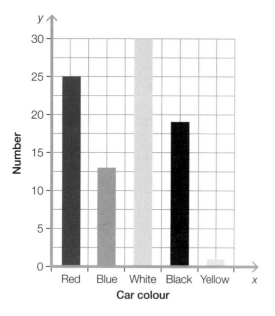

This is a bar chart for the number of pupils at four local schools. The vertical axis is in 100s.

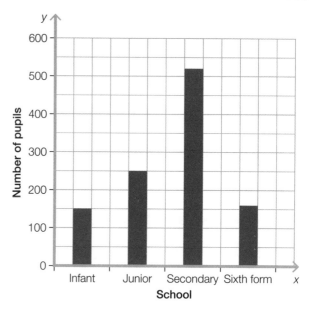

Look at the tables of data. Can you see how each number is shown on the bar chart?

Car colour	Red	Blue	White	Black	Yellow
Number	25	13	30	19	1

Now do the same for the numbers of pupils.

School	Infant	Junior	Secondary	Sixth form
Pupils	150	250	520	160

 **Talk maths**

You could draw a bar chart for favourite colours.

Work with a partner to try to list as many different things that you could make bar charts for. Think of surveys you might do at school or sports that you like.

Discuss what scale you might need to use.

 **check**

A group of friends count the number of books they have at home. Then they make a bar chart. Use the bar chart to answer these questions.

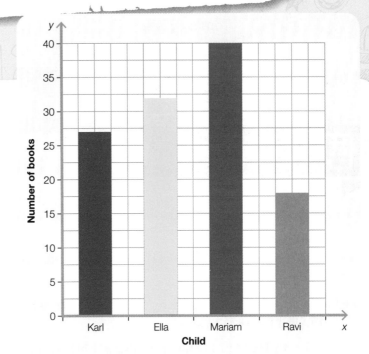

1. Who has the most books?

   _____

2. How many books does Karl have?

   _____

3. How many books are there altogether? _____

4. How many more books does Ella have than Ravi? _____

 **Problems**

Brain-teaser Create a bar chart for the animal lifespan information below. Choose your scale carefully.

Animal	Average lifespan (years)
Elephant	58
Giraffe	24
Lion	17
Rhinoceros	45
Zebra	23

71

Time graphs

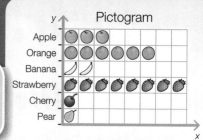

Pictogram

↻ Recap

Each of these graphs has a vertical y-axis and a horizontal x-axis.

We can represent information and data in different types of charts and graphs.

Bar charts and pictograms are useful for presenting information from surveys.

- How do you travel to school?
- What is your favourite snack?
- Do you have any pets?

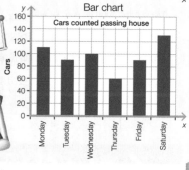

📄 Revise

Time graphs are useful for showing how things change over time, such as temperature changing or things growing.

This graph shows how the temperature changed in the playground during a school day. Look at how you can draw lines to find the temperature at any time of day.

Read the graph to check the table below. Can you read the temperature for 4pm?

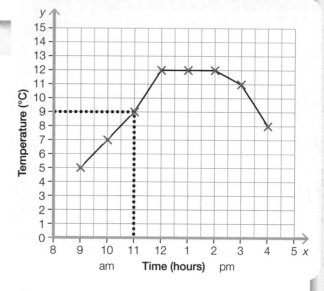

Time	9am	10am	11am	12noon	1pm	2pm	3pm
Temperature	5°C	7°C	9°C	12°C	12°C	12°C	11°C

💡 Tips

- You can create line graphs by plotting points and then joining them.
- This chart shows the height of a tree each year for 5 years.

Time (years)	1	2	3	4	5
Height (metres)	1	3	4	5	5

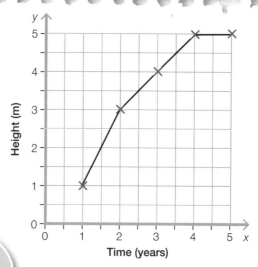

Remember how to plot coordinates: along, and then up.

💬 Talk maths

Working with an adult, use this graph to draw a time graph of your own. (It is OK to invent data rather than find real data.)

- What will the units of time be: seconds, minutes, hours, days, weeks or years?
- What will you show changing in time: a person's height, a baby's weight, the depth of water in a bath, the distance of a bike ride?
- What units will you use for the quantity that is changing: kilograms, litres, kilometres?

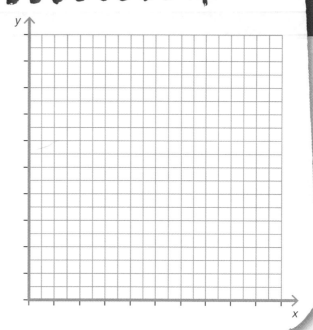

✔ Check

Use the graph opposite to answer these questions.

1. At what time was the water coldest?

   _____

2. When was the water 4°C?

   _____

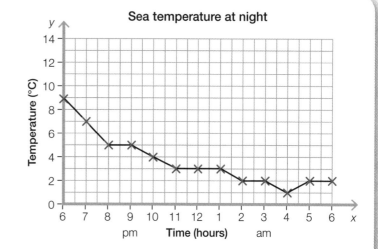

Sea temperature at night

3. Find the difference between the warmest and coldest temperatures. _____

⚠ Problems

Brain-teaser The chart shows a baby's height for the first 6 months. Month '0' is the day the baby was born.

Draw a line graph to show how the baby's height has changed.

Month	0	1	2	3	4	5	6
Height (cm)	37	40	42	46	47	48	50

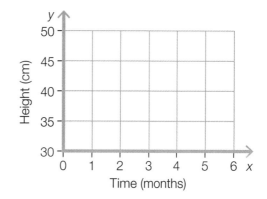

73

Answers: Year 4

NUMBER AND PLACE VALUE

Page 9

1   **a.** seven thousand, three hundred and eighty
      b. two thousand and sixty-nine

2   **a.** 6841   **b.** 5002

3   8 92 250 725 1612 3875 5000 9999

4

1000 more	3350	**2243**	**5789**	**8000**	**9999**
Number	2350	1243	4789	7000	8999
1000 less	1350	**243**	**3789**	**6000**	**7999**

Brain-teaser: **a.** Dipton   **b.** Blinkton
Brain-buster: eleven thousand, two hundred

Page 11

1

	Nearest 10	Nearest 100	Nearest 1000
a. 77	**80**	**100**	**0**
b. 583	**580**	**600**	**1000**
c. 1232	**1230**	**1200**	**1000**
d. 3765	**3770**	**3800**	**4000**

2   **a.** 80   **b.** 70   **c.** 120

3   **a.** 600   **b.** 300   **c.** 1300

4   **a.** 6000   **b.** 4000   **c.** 12,000

Brain-teaser: Blinkton and Mumsford
Brain-buster: 11,000

Page 13

1   **a.** 42, 48, 54, 60   **b.** 63, 70, 77, 84   **c.** 54, 63, 72, 81
     d. 375, 400, 425, 450   **e.** 3000, 4000, 5000, 6000

2   **a.** 78, 72, 66, 60   **b.** 63, 56, 49, 42   **c.** 63, 54, 45, 36
     d. 850, 825, 800, 775   **e.** 8000, 7000, 6000, 5000

Brain-teaser: Joe has £3 more.
Brain-buster: 32 weeks

Page 15

1   **a.** 1   **b.** –1   **c.** –3   **d.** –5   **e.** –5   **f.** –5   **g.** –1   **h.** –6

2   **a.** 2   **b.** 6   **c.** 6

Brain-teaser: –1°C
Brain-buster: 15°C

Page 17

1   **a.** IV   **b.** XI   **c.** XXV   **d.** XIX   **e.** LII   **f.** XLV   **g.** XC   **h.** LXXXVII

2   **a.** 6   **b.** 9   **c.** 17   **d.** 22   **e.** 55   **f.** 40   **g.** 88   **h.** 90

3   0

Brain-teaser: 14 + 23 = 37
Brain-buster: 91 – 65 = 26

CALCULATIONS

Page 19

1   **a.** 50   **b.** 89   **c.** 108   **d.** 394   **e.** 23   **f.** 86   **g.** 95   **h.** 564

2   **a.** 14   **b.** 42   **c.** 44   **d.** 151   **e.** 36   **f.** 61   **g.** 46   **h.** 238

3   **a.** 77   **b.** 99   **c.** 485   **d.** 5838   **e.** 62   **f.** 21   **g.** 133   **h.** 2323

Brain-teaser: **a.** £99   **b.** 105 miles
Brain-buster: £2300

Page 21

1   **a.** 718   **b.** 1003   **c.** 3911   **d.** 7584

2   **a.** 602   **b.** 726   **c.** 8016   **d.** 9619

Brain-teaser: 1850
Brain-buster: 17,014

Page 23

1   **a.** 218   **b.** 425   **c.** 162   **d.** 2818

2   **a.** 179   **b.** 449   **c.** 2605   **d.** 2487

Brain-teaser: **a.** 736   **b.** 111
Brain-buster: 4104

Page 25

1   **a.** 21   **b.** 45   **c.** 32

2   **a.** 4   **b.** 12   **c.** 6

3   0 6 12 18 24 30 36 42 48 54 60 66 72

4   0 12 24 36 48 60 72 84 96 108 120 132 144

5   0 12 24 36 48 60 72

Brain-teaser: 42
Brain-buster: You can say 6 × 9 = 54, and then multiply by 10.
Answer = £5.40

Page 27

1   **a.** 72   **b.** 24   **c.** 950   **d.** 300   **e.** 720   **f.** 1200   **g.** 2400
     h. 9000

2   **a.** 13   **b.** 8   **c.** 15   **d.** 30   **e.** 12   **f.** 3   **g.** 20   **h.** 8

Brain-teaser: **a.** 2400p or £24   **b.** 12
Brain-buster: **a.** 7200p or £72   **b.** 4

Page 29

1   **a.** 114   **b.** 914   **c.** 1368   **d.** 4030

2   **a.** 459   **b.** 534   **c.** 2152   **d.** 7638

Brain-teaser: £10.01 or 1001p
Brain-buster: £33.75 or 3375p

Page 31

1   **a.** 25   **b.** 24   **c.** 18   **d.** 133   **e.** 1167   **f.** 107

2   **a.** 58   **b.** 43   **c.** 142   **d.** 154   **e.** 62   **f.** 103

Brain-teaser: 157
Brain-buster: 552 metres each hour

FRACTIONS AND DECIMALS

Page 33

1 **a.** $\frac{2}{6}$ shaded **b.** $\frac{3}{4}$ shaded **c.** $\frac{4}{10}$ shaded **d.** $\frac{9}{12}$ shaded

2 $\frac{1}{2} = \frac{6}{12}$, $\frac{1}{3} = \frac{4}{12}$, $\frac{1}{4} = \frac{3}{12}$, $\frac{1}{6} = \frac{2}{12}$

3 **a.** $\frac{6}{8}$ **b.** $\frac{6}{9}$ **c.** $\frac{10}{16}$ **d.** $\frac{12}{20}$

Brain-teaser: Jane
Brain-buster: Joe

Page 35

1 **a.** $\frac{1}{2}$ **b.** $\frac{1}{4}$ **c.** $\frac{2}{3}$ **d.** $\frac{4}{7}$

2 **a.** $\frac{1}{2}$ **b.** $\frac{3}{5}$ **c.** $\frac{1}{8}$ **d.** $\frac{7}{20}$

3 **a.** $\frac{5}{4}$ **b.** $\frac{7}{5}$ **c.** $\frac{9}{10}$ **d.** $\frac{11}{8}$ **e.** $\frac{11}{7}$ **f.** $\frac{12}{6}$ or 2

4 **a.** $\frac{4}{3}$ **b.** $\frac{3}{6}$ or $\frac{1}{2}$ **c.** $\frac{6}{8}$ **d.** $\frac{6}{4}$ **e.** $\frac{3}{5}$ **f.** $\frac{13}{20}$

Brain-teaser: $\frac{1}{12}$

Brain-buster: $\frac{11}{20}$

Page 37

1 **a.** $\frac{7}{10}$ **b.** $\frac{12}{10}$ **c.** $\frac{22}{10}$ **d.** $\frac{38}{100}$ **e.** $\frac{81}{100}$ **f.** $\frac{180}{100}$

2 **a.** $\frac{5}{10}$ **b.** $\frac{2}{10}$ **c.** $\frac{14}{10}$ **d.** $\frac{10}{100}$ or $\frac{1}{10}$ **e.** $\frac{52}{100}$ **f.** $\frac{45}{100}$

3 **a.** six tenths **b.** nine tenths **c.** fourteen hundredths
   d. ninety-one hundredths

4 **a.** $\frac{7}{10}$ **b.** $\frac{13}{10}$ **c.** $\frac{35}{100}$ **d.** $\frac{2}{100}$

Brain-teaser: 3 tenths = 30 hundredths
Brain-buster: 63 hundredths = 6 tenths and 3 hundredths

Page 39

1 **a.** 0.5 **b.** 0.25 **c.** 0.75

2 **a.** 0.5 **b.** 0.75 **c.** 0.1 **d.** 0.27 **e.** 0.25 **f.** 0.8

3 **a.** $\frac{1}{4}$ **b.** $\frac{78}{100}$ **c.** $\frac{4}{10}$ **d.** $\frac{3}{4}$ **e.** $\frac{1}{2}$ **f.** $\frac{21}{100}$

Brain-teaser: They are both two tenths.
Brain-buster: She is right, they are both equivalent to 0.75.

Page 41

1 **a.** 0.7 **b.** 0.31 **c.** 0.3 **d.** 0.94

2 **a.** 5 **b.** 3 **c.** 6 **d.** 7

3 **a.** 0.7 < 0.75 **b.** 0.31 < 0.42 **c.** 0.6 = 0.60 **d.** 0.25 > 0.23

4 Decimals should be arranged in this order: 0.05, 0.25, 0.35, 0.5, 0.65, 0.75, 0.9

Brain-teaser: 6.5
Brain-buster: 0.6

MEASUREMENT

Page 43

1 **a.** centimetres **b.** metres **c.** pence **d.** pounds **e.** millilitres
   f. litres **g.** kilograms **h.** grams **i.** minutes or seconds
   j. days or weeks

2 **a.** weighing scales **b.** measuring cylinder **c.** stopwatch

3 **a.** ruler **b.** tape measure **c.** measuring cylinder
   d. weighing scales **e.** stopwatch **f.** calendar

Brain-teaser: 5000g
Brain-buster: 865mm

Page 45

1 2 years = 730 days; 2 weeks = 14 days; 2 days = 48 hours;
   2 hours = 120 minutes; 2 minutes = 120 seconds

2 **a.** 120 seconds **b.** 180 minutes **c.** 96 hours **d.** 35 days
   e. 72 months **f.** 730 days

3 **a.** 210 seconds **b.** 150 minutes **c.** 132 hours **d.** 90 months

Brain-teaser: 3653 days
Brain-buster: **a.** 8760 **b.** 1440

Page 47

1

Analogue	twelve noon	**quarter to nine**	ten past eleven	five to four	**quarter past three**
Digital	**12.00**	8.45	**11.10**	**3.55**	3.15

2 **a.** 01:50 **b.** 16:25 **c.** 06:00 **d.** 23:15

3 **a.** half past eleven am or 11.30am
   b. quarter past three pm or 3.45pm
   c. twenty-five past three am or 3.25am
   d. quarter to one pm or 12.45pm

Brain-teaser: 1 hour and 20 minutes
Brain-buster: 11 hours and 40 minutes

Page 49

1

Pence	500p	150p	3300p	59p	1000p
Pounds	£5	£1.50	£33.00	£0.59	£10.00

2

Pounds	£1	£4.25	£0.62	£20	£12.06
Pence	100p	425p	62p	2000p	1206p

3 **a.** £5.80 **b.** £8.10 **c.** £3.50 **d.** £7.01 **e.** £4 **f.** £10
   e. £5 **h.** £5

Brain-teaser: **a.** £6.25 **b.** £3.75
Brain-buster: **a.** £14.25 **b.** £5.75

Page 51

1 thimble = 20ml, mug = 200ml, bathtub = 200l

2 mouse = 50g, child = 50kg, elephant = 5000kg

3 **a.** 5000g **b.** 6kg **c.** 500g **d.** $4\frac{1}{2}$kg or 4.5kg

4 **a.** 3l **b.** 7500ml **c.** $3\frac{1}{2}$l or 3.5l **d.** 500ml

5 **a.** $3\frac{3}{4}$kg or 3.75kg **b.** 1150g **c.** 420g **d.** 3700ml **e.** 0.37l
   f. 5000ml

Brain-teaser: **a.** 20 **b.** 2kg and 700g
Brain-buster: **a.** 25 **b.** 8

Page 53

1 **a.** 50mm **b.** 30mm **c.** 45mm **d.** 27mm

2 **a.** 4cm **b.** 7cm **c.** 6.3cm

3 **a.**

mm	cm
10	1
100	10
20	2
350	35
1000	100

b.

cm	m
100	1
1000	10
25	0.25
50	0.5
1000	10

c.

m	km
500	$\frac{1}{2}$
2000	2
250	$\frac{1}{4}$
1000	1
9000	9

Brain-teaser: 1.54m or 154cm
Brain-buster: $9\frac{1}{2}$km or 9.5km or 9500m

Page 55

1 **a.**
   length 4cm, width 2cm
   perimeter = 12cm

   b.
   side length 3cm
   perimeter = 12cm

2 **a.** 8cm **b.** 8cm **c.** 12cm

3

Shape	Length	Height	Perimeter
rectangle	5cm	2cm	**14cm**
rectangle	12mm	5mm	**34mm**
rectangle	6km	2km	**16km**
square	8mm	8mm	**32mm**
square	5m	5m	**20m**
square	4.5cm	4.5cm	**18cm**

Brain-teaser: 14km

1   **a.** 6 squares   **b.** 16 squares   **c.** 5 squares   **d.** 12 squares

2   **a.** 12 squares   **b.** 9 squares

Brain-teaser: The area of the rectangle is 20 squares greater than the square.

Brain-buster: 10 blocks

GEOMETRY

Page 58

1   **a.** acute   **b.** obtuse   **c.** right angle

2   **a.** 3   **b.** 4   **c.** 2   **d.** 1

Brain-teaser: They make a straight line, which is two right angles.

Page 59

1   **a.** Right-angled   **b.** Isosceles   **c.** Equilateral   **d.** Scalene

Brain-teaser:

There are various possibilities. The isosceles triangle must have two sides of the same length; and the scalene must have sides that are all different lengths.

Page 61

1   A square has sides that are all the same length, whereas a rectangle only has opposite sides of equal length.

2   All the sides of a rhombus are the same length, whereas only adjacent sides are equal on a kite.

3   A parallelogram has two pairs of parallel sides, whereas a trapezium only has one pair of parallel sides.

4

a. Trapezium	**b.** Parallelogram	**c.** Kite	**d.** Rhombus

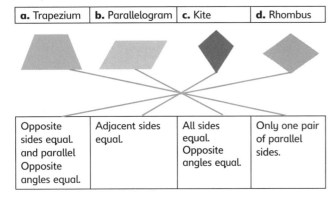

Opposite sides equal. and parallel Opposite angles equal.	Adjacent sides equal.	All sides equal. Opposite angles equal.	Only one pair of parallel sides.

Brain-teaser: A square or a rhombus

Brain-buster: It is possible. Check that the sketch shows the right angle at the top of the kite, with equal sides in the correct places.

1

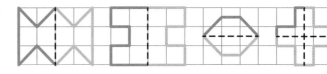

2

3

Brain-teaser:

Brain-buster: H I O X

Page 65

1   **a.** X = (3, 4), Y = (7, 5)

    b. Check that a square has been plotted with these coordinates: A (2, 2), B (2, 8), C (8, 8), D (8, 2)

2   **a.** P = (2, 2), Q = (3, 6), R = (6, 3)

    b. Check that a rectangle has been plotted with these coordinates: J (1, 1), K (9, 1), L (9, 7), M (1, 7)

Brain-teaser: (7, 5)

Page 67

1   **a.** Check that the points have been plotted correctly.

    b. W = (9, 1), X = (6, 2), Y = (5, 0), Z = (4, 4)

2   **a.** Check that a triangle has been plotted correctly at these coordinates: A (2, 2), B (4, 4), C (4, 2)

    b. Check that a triangle has been plotted correctly at these coordinates: A = (5, 7), B = (7, 9), C = (7, 7)

    c. A = (5, 7), B = (7, 9), C = (7, 7)

Brain teaser: 5 left, 4 down

STATISTICS
Page 69

1. Check that the pictogram has been drawn correctly.

2. **a.** elephant **b.** lion and zebra **c.** giraffe and zebra
   d. 180cm **e.** 300kg **f.** 6 years

Brain-teaser: lion and zebra

Page 71

1. Mariam

2. 27

3. 117

4. 14

Brain-teaser: Check that the bar chart has been drawn correctly.

Page 73

1. 4am

2. 10pm

3. 8°C

Brain-teaser: Check that the time graph has been drawn correctly.

Glossary

12-hour clock Uses 12 hours, with am before 12 noon, and pm after.

24-hour clock Uses 24 hours for the time; does not need am or pm, 17:30 = 5:30pm.

2D Two-dimensional, a flat shape like a square.

A

Acute angle An angle smaller than one right angle.

Adjacent Near or next to something, usually used for talking about angles, sides or faces.

Analogue clock Shows the time with hands on a clock face.

Angle A measure of turn, for example a right angle.

Anti-clockwise Rotating in the opposite direction to the hands of a clock.

Approximate A number found by rounding or estimating.

Area The amount of surface covered by a shape.

Axis (plural axes) The horizontal and vertical lines on a graph.

B

Bar chart A chart that uses bars of different heights to represent data.

C

Clockwise Rotating in the same direction as the hands of a clock.

Column addition/subtraction Arranging numbers in place-value columns to make addition easier.

Coordinates Numbers that give the position of a point on a coordinate grid, (x, y).

D

Decimal A number less than 1, shown with digits and a decimal point.

Decimal places The numbers to the right of the decimal point, such as tenths, hundredths.

Decimal point The dot used to separate the whole number part of a decimal from the part that is less than 1.

Denominator The number on the bottom of a fraction.

Difference The amount between two numbers.

Digits Our number system uses ten digits, 0–9, to represent all our numbers.

Digital clock Shows time using digits rather than by having hands on a clock face.

E

Equivalent fractions The same amount represented differently, such as $\frac{1}{2}$ and $\frac{2}{4}$.

Estimate To use information to get an approximate answer.

Even numbers Numbers that can be divided by 2. They end in 0, 2, 4, 6 or 8.

I

Irregular polygon A 2D shape which does not have identical sides and angles.

L

Line of symmetry Parts of a symmetrical shape are mirror images of each other either side of a line symmetry.

M

Mental methods Approaches for accurately solving calculations without writing them down.

N

Negative number A number less than zero.

Numerator The top number of a fraction. The numerator is divided by the denominator.

O

Obtuse angle An angle larger than one right angle and smaller than two right angles.

Odd numbers Numbers that cannot be divided by 2. They end in 1, 3, 5, 7 or 9.

P

Partitioning Breaking down numbers into 1000s, 100s, 10s and 1s, to make calculations easier

Perimeter The distance around the edge of a closed shape.

Pictogram A chart that uses pictures to represent data.

Q

Quadrilateral A flat shape with four sides, such as rhombus, square, rectangle, kite, parallelogram, trapezium.

R

Regular shape A 2D shape with all sides the same length and all angles the same size.

Right angle A quarter turn.

Roman numerals The system of letters used by the Romans to represent numbers.

Rounding Simplifying numbers to the nearest 10, 100 and so on.

S

Symbol A sign used for an operation or relationship in mathematics, such as +, −, ×, ÷, =, < or >.

Symmetrical A symmetrical shape is one that is identical either side of a line of symmetry.

T

Time graph Used to show how something changes over time, such as height, temperature or speed.

Translation Moving the coordinates of points or shapes by the same amounts on a graph.

Triangle A 2D shape with three sides. Can be equilateral, isosceles, right-angled or scalene.

Multiplication table

x	1	2	3	4	5	6	7	8	9	10	11	12
1	1	2	3	4	5	6	7	8	9	10	11	12
2	2	4	6	8	10	12	14	16	18	20	22	24
3	3	6	9	12	15	18	21	24	27	30	33	36
4	4	8	12	16	20	24	28	32	36	40	44	48
5	5	10	15	20	25	30	35	40	45	50	55	60
6	6	12	18	24	30	36	42	48	54	60	66	72
7	7	14	21	28	35	42	49	56	63	70	77	84
8	8	16	24	32	40	48	56	64	72	80	88	96
9	9	18	27	36	45	54	63	72	81	90	99	108
10	10	20	30	40	50	60	70	80	90	100	110	120
11	11	22	33	44	55	66	77	88	99	110	121	132
12	12	24	36	48	60	72	84	96	108	120	132	144